OLD
LACE & LINENS
Including
CROCHET
An Identification and Value Guide

by
Maryanne Dolan

BOOKS AMERICANA INC

ISBN 0-89689-072-4

ACKNOWLEDGEMENTS:

Thank you   Marlys Aboudara
Virginia Cox
Pearline Munson
Linda Shaw
Catherine Smith
Betty Williamson
and to Roger P. Woodhour of the Quaker Lace Company for his interest and cooperation.

For the Carroll sisters

Who loved them and collected them
but never made them.

AUTHOR'S NOTE

Collectors may dream of owning a Point de Venice shawl or a ball gown with an overskirt of Mechlin; we visit museums and sigh over such lavish display; we read of those long-ago beauties with low decollete with elegant trim and flounced hems of exquisite embroidery, we visualize ourselves living among the monumental tapestries and handsome draperies of days gone by, but when our practical selves intrude on this delightful fantasy we usually find ourselves in the small shops devoted to vintage materials and clothing or trying to pry some fine scraps of lace out of Great Aunt Honoria – even haunting the flea markets and garage sales for overlooked bits and pieces.

The quest itself is a marvelous diversion and sometimes we find the pot of gold or its equivalent – a colorful embroidered cloth of purest, softest linen.

The days when we could acquire lace or embroidery work of great antiquity, or linens soft and sensuous of a size large enough to grace a long table, at a low price are long gone. Museums have coveted and acquired them and wise collectors, ahead of their time, took these materials to their bosom. Literally, for many an ordinary dress or undergarment has graduated to 'original' status with desirable additions of older lace or embroidery trim.

Today's collectors are a different breed. We treasure the hand made lace or the hand sewn quilt or cloth for its own sake. We do long for the things we can probably never own and while it is lovely to learn about the truly valuable heirloom materials in our past, it is essential that we live in the real world where for the most part such grandiose things are the province of museums or wealthy collectors. The newly established retail trade in older vintage materials offers competition for what is available as does the whole new generation of interested collectors. Vintage Clothing of much that we cherish in lace, linen, embroidery, as well as older fabrics, is already one of the fastest growing collecting areas.

Nothing is impossible though. At a large flea market I recently found what must surely be an 18th century narrow shawl with its gold and silver thread muted but its delicious embroidery designs still glowing and spreading joy with their beauty. People not the least bit interested in needlework admire it.

This quest, this searching is most exhilerating. Who knows what may lurk around that next collecting corner.

We are concerned here with what is readily available and affordable.

No frustration is greater than seeking that which is not really there.

Maryanne Dolan
138 Belle Avenue
Pleasant Hill, CA 94523

INTRODUCTION

It is relatively easy to collect Grandma's linens and laces. They still surface at flea markets, garage sales and lately shops have begun to feature them in a dignified way. They are at least no longer relegated to boxes in the backroom which customers would rummage through at will and buy for a pittance. They are sold regularly at the best antique shows – these linens and laces, these embroideries and antimacassars and doilies. A whole new segment of the collecting world is now seeking them. Prices are going up in a rather alarming way.

There have always been those who treasured these reminders of how Grandma lived, how she protected her chairs and tables, how Mother decorated her dresser, how Great Grandma spent hour upon hour with her needlework which now is considered a priceless heirloom.

Because of the quantities in which they were made and because of the early collectors, the smaller pieces survive in great numbers; the tablecloths and runner and napkins are still available but competition is widening and prices reflect this interest.

The trend started late in a general way; after all these bits and pieces are a true and definitive statement on the way people lived and decorated but it is probably the disenchantment with shoddy workmanship and our throwaway world which has escalated the value of this new collectible.

About 20 years ago I purchased an estate which included several sets of quite beautiful, delicate Victorian collar and cuff sets of different types of lace. There was no real interest and finally these wonderful treasures were bought by an elderly customer for her own use. Her daughter inherited the sets, does not wear them but has had them framed and hung in her bedroom. A marvelous commentary on the way we have developed as a nation of conservators, how we have come to appreciate not only workmanship and materials, but what these linens and laces and Vintage whites mean to us, what we can learn from them.

The astute collector is always in the vanguard of what ultimately becomes a fad, the younger collectors are now avidly seeking the best of the old whites, using them in imaginative ways and so preserving them for the future. The passion for early Americana and the 'country' look is a contributing factor

1

in the new popularity of old linens – the feeling of 'home and hearth' which has infected us all.

This book is intended to interest you the collector, to whet your appetite for the things many grew up with and took for granted, and for those who have encountered them only recently and are intrigued; for anyone interested in the art of needlework and often it is indeed a fine art. For anyone who can see beyond these little white squares or rounds to what they meant to those who made them and used them, to anyone who admires beauty in whatever form.

The wonderful world of Vintage Whites is unstructured, collect whatever suits your fancy – all of it is useful, most of it is lovely and much of it is pure fun.

VICTORIAN ERA

The Victorians were incredible. In this plastic age it is difficult for us to identify with a people who decorated everything with a fussiness alien to our way of life. Everything possible was adorned; their homes, their clothing, their persons, their tables. Not for them, a table set with simple mats or a plain tablecloth. Not for them, a table set simply with an uncomplicated centerpiece. No indeed. The table usually boasted a cloth of embroidered linen or ornate lace. Together with their endless pieces of silver and the various table accoutrements deemed necessary to their dining happiness, the whole looked overdone and fussy. Taken separately that cloth of linen or lace was often quite beautifully made, a minor work of art. They used them, they made them or paid dearly for them and we ignored them for a long time. Scorned them, in fact, and only recently have we begun eagerly to seek them.

The needlework of the Victorians is a definitive delineation of their way of life. As we find and buy these often small pieces owned by the Victorian lady, let's reflect on her lifestyle.

She was circumscribed as to behavior and in her social life; it was a rare woman of that day who worked outside of her home which was the center of her life; her clothing hampered her activities which is probably why much of her life was sedentary. Her life was directed by the men in it and they and she subscribed to the theory that idle hands were the devil's workshop. She certainly must have thought as she worked, but was not in general introspective. She was often revered by the men in her life and was considered the center of the home, but her freedoms were curtailed and often in the needlework we see expressions of creativity stifled in other areas of her life. Her needlework was often exquisite, learned early from her mother or perhaps an aunt. She worked at it diligently, it was considered ladylike and genteel. She enjoyed it and was proud of it, these qualities are evident and help make is so dear to us today. Magazines were devoted to it – the periodicals of the day talked endlessly of patterns and materials, letters to the editor flew back and forth in great numbers, sales by retailers and wholesalers were brisk. It was a consuming activity. The attitude is probably one we would not fully understand as we dash off to the golf course or drive children to the swim meet or rush off to the office.

3

To us needlework in any guise is intended to be an interlude of relaxation, to the Victorian woman it was an integral part of daily life. That is why there is so much available to collectors. There are still mounds of it hiding in attics, there are untapped treasures in myriad trunks and boxes, some of it long forgotten and mouldering away. A family member tells of her most vivid and comforting memory – watching her grandmother piece together one of the quilts she seemed always to be making. "A vigorous, vibrant woman," she says, "of great intelligence and energy and also great skill." It is these characteristics which those women put into their needlework which makes it so collectible and it is truly amazing how their patterns and designs fit into our homes today. Not only is so much of their work beautiful but the fact that so much of it is completely hand done lends it a value we can now appreciate.

Very few of us have the time anymore to spend long periods edging sheets and pillowcases or embroidering or making lace. Certainly in a sense we have lost something – it must have been a reassuring sight to come upon these women at the work/hobby; needle in, needle out. Mother was in her place and all was right with the world.

How the women themselves felt is not so clearly documented. They were certainly proud of their work and used it to decorate their homes and their persons.

It was a different world which spawned the things we now collect so avidly, but women were emerging, or beginning to, and there would be less time for the wonderful handwork, homework if you will, that these women did. Children were seen but not heard and girls were taught needlework at an early age. It is quite endearing to see some of the lesser efforts of younger girls, the embroidery stitches will be crooked, the applique not consistent, the knitting less than perfect. The humanity of the workmanship becomes evident and thought provoking. Such examples are usually not collected. I find them entirely charming and if the colors and shapes appeal, always buy them. These are usually found in smaller sized pieces on which the beginners worked, the handmade tablecloths of highly colored embroidery, the tapestries, the laces, are the product of more skilled hands.

In the late 1800s women were being chastised by the editor of a popular ladies magazine, "It is alarming how few wives and mothers are interested or have any knowledge of the science

4

of domesticity." At the same time the magazine was also saying, "Surely the making of doilies, of tablecovers and of pillows, like the making of books, seem to have no end." Needlework was considered a gentle art and while women may have begun to rebel in small ways, forsaking the needle arts was not one of them.

The fertile brain has always been soothed by working with the hands. Many of these highly intelligent women formed sewing clubs and worked in tandem on projects (often with worthy goals) which allowed them social intercourse, a release for their creativity and at the same time established their social status. Some of these women had sufficient wealth to ignore ordinary household cares so they could spend the huge amounts of time some of the projects demanded. It is largely to the leisure class of women that we owe many of the elaborate, spectacular large bedspreads, tablecloths, tapestries and other superb pieces which are now rapidly rising in price so that we are hardly able to afford them. In this collecting field haste is the watchword.

All women though worked with their needles. They competed with each other to do the finest work, often the competition was subtle within a social group since much of the result of their effort was used in their homes, but there were places where competitions were held on a more honest basis, such as fairs and bazaars and all the entries were the pride of the entrants. There was an incredible number of bazaars, there were untold 'societies' and 'groups' somewhat on the order of the old quilting bee. Most of the designs they used were traditional, flowers, birds, landscapes, but some show great originality. In the mid-Victorian period Berline work or needlepoint was enormously popular, since it was colorful and not too difficult to do. This is now becoming prohibitively expensive as it enjoys a lively revival.

Women right this minute are creating the antique needlework of the future, although today's needlewoman does not usually have the time for the scope of the Victorian and what we see is often merely background work on designs already done.

Folk Art Actions are beginning to feature this later American needlework. The pieces which incorporate the traditional eagle or farm scenes; samplers, landscapes, all sell well. The very early samplers have long commanded extremely high prices and it is a wise collector who looks for the samplers of a later day, those made by girls from the late Victorian period well into the 1930s. It is a fertile collecting field with a sure appreciation of your investment – not only money-wise but for sheer enjoyment. You will probably never be able to part with any you manage to buy.

Life which changed dramatically during the Victorian years and one change which affected the sewing projects was the introduction of the table lamp. It seems as nothing to us today but in the Victorian psyche a genie was stirring. The new lamp could not just stand there on a highly polished table – no indeed, it called for more doilies or a runner or a scarf; and needlework reached a new plateau of more homely (and homey) practicality. And we are the beneficiaries. These are primarily the things we covet today. The Victorian center table or side table would have been crammed with all sorts of objects, and all of them sitting in profusion on a hand-worked table cover. So many tables with so many covers have left us a bonanza, and with prices still reasonable because of abundance the collector still has a great variety of choice. It's a dream world if you love needlework but the situation is bound to change soon.

Many of these charming smaller pieces are framed by collectors and lend a nostalgic air to any wall. Antimacassars are beloved of collectors and sometimes used. Their original purpose was a sensible one and since they are easily cared for and laundered we are delighted when we see them in place on chairs or sofas looking right at home. Pillows and cushions are often elaborate even magnificent with their variety of stitchery and imaginative designs. The materials from which these are sometimes made can be extravagant. Most are still usable and add a highly decorative touch. Since we are not quite in the mode of Victorian clutter, care should be taken so that such elaborate needlework does not overpower the furnishings in the room.

Beloved of antique shop owners, decorators and many collectors are the mottoes. Recently I saw an example depicting a slightly peculiar looking eagle standing guard over a needlework ''God Bring Us Safely Home.'' Although this was done in vivid colors on velvet there are many similar exhortations available. Some in wool on perforated cardboard and appropriately framed in keeping with the period are delightful. These framed mottoes are generally much more expensive than the bits and pieces we can discover in shops. It is passing strange that what was once so commonplace is eagerly sought after today actually coveted and put in a place of honor. The collecting wheel has come full circle regarding the Victorian fancies. Our quest of the needlework is a commentary of how life changes and moves on but the collecting heart always feels the need to go home again. Needlework has ever been popular with women, and some men, although its expression has altered and although it faded from favor it never expired completely and today it is a much-loved pastime.

That these Victorian pieces have a certain charm cannot be denied. Sometimes they are truly beautiful, often they are like the women themselves, over sentimental and effusive beyond our lifestyles. 'Welcome To This Humble Abode' reads a framed motto now hanging in an upscale ranch house; strange looking animals gambol on a small tapestry – what did that woman have in mind? – the everlasting symbol of Victoriana, the child standing mourning by the tombstone, graces another needlework square. The accompanying hair picture seems appropriate and is, of course, another expensive collectible. But then there is the wonderful embroidered bedspread made in 1897 applique still remarkably bright and entertaining – 2 knights jousting in 1897? The colorful threads alone would be worth the price.

Today with the emphasis on restoration, Victorian homes are being carefully nurtured back to their original state and the purist requires original or period furniture and needlework to complement the homes themselves. This is one reason the elegant gracious lace curtains are disappearing from the marketplace. They are now so difficult to find that several companies are making reproductions out of new materials. The Quaker Lace Company, still using the Nottingham looms from days of long ago, is producing the curtains made with polyester and cotton. Rue de France sells by catalogue and there are others in the mail order field. It is a big market.

There is something very romantic and airy about these older lace designs. They are not easy to find but diligent collectors do occasionally come upon a pair, but will certainly settle for a single panel. The inventive mind can find many uses for such workmanship as is evidenced in the older lace. In the renewed passion for Victoriana do not overlook the precious embroideries of the period, they lend themselves in a particular way to our return to the mildly cluttered look now prevailing in decorating circles.

Exquisite embroidery work flourished in the transitional years between the Victorian and the roaring 20s. William Morris was bringing change to the decorating world with his 'beautiful but functional and simple' philosophy. His dictum brought immediate changes in needlework design.

At last recognized for what it is, a gigantic last gasp of the individual artisan, the so-called 'arts and crafts' movement produced linens of such distinction they are fast gaining stature and rising in price as they become more scarce. The work is referred to as 'art embroidery' and is highly distinguished because it was made specifically to harmonize with the furniture of the period.

Everyone has heard of, or remembers, the Morris chair. Almost all homes in Great Grandmother's day had such a chair and its angular style required a certain kind of decorative needlework to soften its rather masculine lines. This was a rather exciting time when individual crafts flourished. The attitude manifested itself in the needlework – magnificent, often complicated wall hangings, now quite costly – but there are the usual more mundane things done in an unusual way, the table runner, cushion covers – almost anything which could be embroidered. Book covers would be a marvelous collectible from this era.

It is rather difficult for us today, living as we do with washable, non-wrinkle fabrics even in tablecloths, and with little time for the involved needlework necessary, to appreciate the enormous pride women took in such little things, seeking out and matching threads exactly, in looking for and choosing patterns to suit their angular furniture, in spending hours, even days or weeks, embroidering tapestries which were often displayed as works of art, the way a good painting might be treasured today. Women were justifiably proud of their work, so many pieces were signed. Names of the most talented, and the movers and shakers of the sewing guilds have been recorded and are now revered. Silk embroidery of the day is so expert and lovely it seems a pity to actually use some of the work – definitely it is art.

This whole stitchery craze was a large movement in its day. Names such as Louis Tiffany involved himself to the extent of forming the "Society of Decorative Arts." Other well-known artisans lent prestige to these groups and a rather significant avant-garde segment of the artistic world became enmeshed. The results of the work of these people who banded together for the sole purpose of doing fine needlework are truly wonderful, if slightly esoteric to the untrained eye. They are expensive, sought after with great energy by a smallish number of collectors. More collectors should be aware of linens of this period, they are not yet fully understood and bargains can still be had. An investment.

For the average women, not dealing with the best of the artist designed furniture of the day but more likely living in a home furnished with the best (or worst) of Grand Rapids Oak, Mission style, the needlework was on a more modest scale. Although the beautifully made and creatively designed and executed tapestries with their silk threads can be found and purchased, it is the small examples of the work of more humble origin that we can most easily find. Even these are rising rapidly in price. As the Arts and Crafts period gains new converts and more publicity leads to better understanding of the style and the patterns, this needlework which is often more handsome than beautiful (except in its workmanship) will continue to surface. Much is either still in hiding, or perhaps it was not made in such great abundance, and then, too, it is not always recognized for what it is.

It is, generally speaking, embroidery done in bright colors in applique fashion. The making of it became a major passion with many woman's groups and many wealthy patrons commissioned designs for their grand homes. It was all rather in a much older manner, this sort of patronage is not often practiced today. The famous Lily Langtry was a great fan of the needlework and well known millionaires filled their homes with the needlework of the Arts and Crafts Sewing Societies. For the most part, the old mansions or museums are the repositories of the best of the work. The whole emphasis was on good design and striking impact.

The Victorian era with its over-ornamentation was anathema to these people who followed the dictates of William Morris, and the current popularity of the work as reflected in auction prices definitely points to this period as a prime collecting field. The Frank Lloyd Wright artifacts, the work of Gustav Stickley all are coming into their own. Wright built and furnished with a unique version for a particular landscape, and the needlework needed to enhance that vision.

That is one of the rare qualities of the needlework, it was amazingly in tune with the vision of the men who dictated the evolution of the period and the women who understood this

~ designed and created the impressive needlework with such empathy. The Bostom Museum of Fine Arts played a major role in this deveopment and was one of its earliest exponents. Today most of the large museums have examples of this period needlework and all needlework lovers should view it. It has a characteristic look that once seen in a collection it thereafter becomes almost always recognizeable.

The frivolous among us are tremendously amused by much of the needlework of the 1920s and 1930s. As with every period there was a quantity of beautiful, careful needlework done by serious stitchers. But those hand towels with their flappers, or stylized basket of flowers, the kitchen scenes, the kittens chasing a ball of yarn, the typical colonial ladies decorating hundreds of bedspreads – all of it is great fun and shows surprisingly proficient workmanship.

Tons of it was simple embroidery on stamped material. If today we think we are besieged by ads and commercials on every hand, the women of those years were equally bombarded in every newspaper and magazine by manufacturers of stamped materials, of threads and sewing items, of edgings of all kinds. Guilt feelings must have been overwhelming if one did not like the needlework arts.

In the 1930s women were entertained by radio personalties discussing sewing and related topics and in fact during the deep depression sewing on a mundane scale became a necessity for many. One of the qualities which makes the 1930s simple needlework so appealing is the original use of the piece. We can easily visualize the need for the furniture chairbacks or arm covers, we are close enough to understand it. No one wants to dwell on those often unhappy years, but in the collecting world, on many levels and in many different areas, it has become prime time. Poetic justice perhaps that those women, struggling against financial difficulty and lack of much social life, produced so much that is whimsical. It is a tribute to fortitude and courage of high order.

Needlework, good and bad, has endured forever. The renewed interest by collectors proves that a love of beauty is inherent, that a respect for skill by the artisan endures long after she has finished her work. We collectors gratefully acknowledge the past while bringing it into the present and preserving it for the future.

LINEN

When we consider the world of antiquities we think of pot shards, of crude glass, of stone tools, of mummified figures. Linen? Almost never, yet it is linen that is mentioned in the Bible, for thousands of years before the Christian era linen was being made and worn in Egypt. In Greece and Rome linen was regularly worn, the spinning of flax being an ordinary household task. Then it was done with spindles which changed little for centuries and when the spinning wheel was finally developed it was considered a marvel. The old spinning wheels so graceful and sculpturally beautiful, are now collected for themselves, if not always for use by needlework purists. With the eventual arrival of machines for spinning some of the artistry of the work lessened but the linen itself became more easily available and consequently less expensive.

The early process of making linen fabric seems almost unbelievable to us now. The whorls were of bone or stone or terra cotta, the spindle which was of wood was put through a hole in the center and the whorl with its heavy weight gave impetus to the spindle when twirling to twist the flax. The Egyptian flax has survived because of the sand and dry atmosphere. So linen immediately has status – it is an ancient material, still popular after ages of use, still desirable in any of its guises or of any age. In truth, linen is ageless.

Linen has always had a certain aura. Longwearing, it proved to be a boon to women who kept the family clothed and warm, fashionables have kept it in the forefront, particularly the Edwardians; endless tables have been set with it. Linen does everything and goes everywhere. It always has.

Its only drawback is its proclivity to crease. The word itself – linen – has an heirloom ring to it and those fortunate enough to own linen from the past which has descended in families know full well they own something fine and valuable.

Linen is remarkably long lasting although frequent launderings may weaken the fibers and eventually the piece may tear. Linen is prone to stress. Tablecloths, for example, are subject to small damage from interaction with the flatware. As with anything else which has been used over a long period of time the minute tears in an already weakened fabric will worsen so should be mended immediately, although as with the silver which caused them, they take on new character with slight imperfections.

One of the lures of old linen is the soft, almost caressable feeling it takes on from having been handled and used over a period of time, it is partly what makes it collectible.

Some linens show signs of having been starched too much, too often and then folded so that the fold lines are almost permanent. Over-starching is one of the great negatives in dealing with linen, sometimes pieces can be found which will almost stand upright alone because of stiffness. In the past (and even now some new collectors do this) people took one look at linen and immediately thought 'starch.' Here is a case of too much of a good thing.

Pure, untreated linen is becoming rather scarce since with new techniques the material can be made to withstand its nemesis, creasing. The new approach makes it more desirable as a clothing material and most other everyday uses, but to collectors it does rob the fabric of some of its integrity. But linen with its long history seems never to go out of style; the very name inspires a sense of confidence and elegance and not even the most beautiful of the man-made fibers has ever eclipsed the pride a hostess feels when she knows her table is set with a magnificent glowing linen cloth while she herself might receive in an equally stunning Vintage linen gown.

Irish linen has always been, and continues to be, the label which attracts astute collectors. It was, and sometimes still is, made by hand and it is wondrously light. Ireland has a damp climate and good, rich soil – ideal for growing the flax. Ireland then Belgium are the chief exporters of fine linen today.

Linen is made from flax fibers which have a smooth surface. There are several types including the type used for tablecloths and napkins which has a damask weave. Today much of the harvesting and combing is done by machine but if the linen is made by the same age-old process is still used. Probably the best old linens were made from which which is considered the superior fiber because it is lint free and beautifully shaded in tones of buff or white. Linen has so many marvelous qualities it quite overshadows most other materials but one of its greatest properties is its strength, hence its durability.

The Egyptians used linen to wrap their dead, among other things. To this day much of that linen survives intact because the flax from which it was made was very high quality. For centuries the ways or producing that linen remained unchanged and during the Middle Ages most of Europe cultivated flax. Linen has been a part of life seemingly forever.

When we speak of linen we generally think of one kind of fabric, but in actuality linen ranges from very heavy to very fine. All fanciers of vintage clothing are familiar with the terms butcher linen, cambric and huckaback. These are varieties of linen, the cambric most often used in clothing, the huckaback was used for linen towels because it has an unusually high ability to absorb moisture.

The damask tablecloths and napkins so in favor today, that competition for the older examples is becoming a race, is really linen damask woven on a Jacquard loom.

One of the difficult linen cloths to find is the large oval or round type, the square cloths were obviously made in great numbers. While we also find older examples of linen sheets and pillowcases collectors now seem to buy these for reasons other than sleeping on, or under. All of the older pure linens are becoming costly.

Part of the price increase, for things that not too long ago could have been picked up for the proverbial song, is the realization that they represent a dying craft, and the revival of interest and the resultant search for things that are hand made. The process of making linen was never an easy one and the finished product even then could not have been sold too cheaply.

The flax itself is a fibrous plant which must first be taken out of the ground. Originally this was always done by hand, pulled up root and all. It then had to be cured and dried in the open, then combed – a process which removed all the seed and leaves from the stalk. The next step – 'retting' probably a derivation of the word 'rotting' since that is precisely what is meant to happen. The bundles are left to partially rot so the fibers can be easily loosened from the stem. There is no such thing as instant rotting. The process takes up to a month.

The reason the Irish linen is so fine is not only the quality of the flax itself but because all the steps were done carefully by hand. Part of the tedious process was standing careful guard over the stalks while they ferment in a moving stream. Considering what went into its making the old linen is a bargain at any price. There are many more steps before the flax reached our table in its metamorphosis as a gorgeous tablecloth. Combing is a long procedure, which is called 'hacking' during which the long soft linen fibers are separated from the short, not-so-fine ones. A series of metal combs are used and as the linen fibers are constantly worked to produce only the finest, the combs have more teeth than the preceding ones. The combs themselves are a wonderful collectible although I have never seen such a collection in private hands. There is the sliver, the roving, and it is only after many, many involved steps which are much condensed here that we have the woven linen fabric. The trend now is to substitute chemicals for some of the steps formerly done by hand so much linen will never achieve the excellence or have the unique characteristics of the old. Collectors need to be alert for possibilities, many people are not aware of what they have. The collector always needs to be.

All good collectors know the very finest things in life are well worth the effort. Thus it is with linen; in this fabric we have history, we have unexcelled beauty with utility. We can own something, which if properly cared for, can continue to be or may become a genuine valuable heirloom. Linen is lovely.

Living With Linens

Living with linen is a joy but as with other fine things it requires some care. Laundering should be done carefully in warm water with a mild non-abrasive soap. Fels – Naptha brand has been used successfully by connoisseurs for a long time. Nowadays almost any good, non-abrasive detergent will do the job. For small pieces, many collectors wash linens in the kitchen sink or a deep container; for large tablecloths or vintage clothes, try the bathtub. To remove stains try lemon juice and salt on the dampened cloth, then dry in the sun until the stain is bleached.

I must confess to having used an excellent French laundry which for many years served my linens well. Time marches on and the French laundry has disappeared so I will revert to tried and true methods of caring for linen.

After washing try drying the linens in the sun, spread out in the sun over absorbent towels. Never add crease marks by folding in familiar creases. In fact after the piece has been carefully ironed roll it rather than fold it. A hot iron must be used (carefully) and if you desire starch, try spraying lightly.

If linens are in fairly regular use unusual care need not be taken, ordinary good sense will dictate what needs to be done. Old remedies for stains talk of ''soap jelly'' which works best ''but probably soap flakes work out better.'' They also recommend a 15 minute pre-soak in lukewarm water to loosen soil. My grandmother suggested a dose of buttermilk to remove the yellowish tinge, but an old time laundry worker has advised me that when blueing went out of fashion, linen could be revived by dipping in oxalic acid which had been dissolved, then all would be rinsed. It's interesting to read of remedies and methods from the past, for the present taking care of our precious linens is not that complicated – common sense and not too much starch.

EMBROIDERY

Think of the Caliph Moctadi at the beginning of the 9th century living in a palace in which were hung 38,000 pieces of tapestry – 12,500 of which were embroidered with gold. Try to imagine such opulence, acknowledge the great skill and taste of the Eastern embroiderers and then set out to search for Great Grandma's antimacassars.

The needlework arts have resurfaced after generations of eclipse and we, the collectors, as well as those who follow are going to be enriched by our habits of preservation. We are going to have the fun of seeking out those pieces which interest us, which may or may not be perfect in their proportions or execution but which please us in their uniqueness.

It is all a far cry from the early 19th century notion ''that it must be a delightful entertainment for the fair sex, whom their native modesty and the tenderness of men toward them exempts them from public business, to pass their hours in imitating fruits and flowers and transplanting all the beauties of nature into their dress or decorations for their apartments.'' Someone actually said that and indeed it was the prevailing attitude of the day. Now women use embroidery to relax, or enjoy themselves in searching for pieces they want. Needlework, especially the embroideries, have become the newest, fastest rising collectible. It is a thing of beauty which will last almost forever if well cared for. And it is for the most part the result of the way women decorated their homes and their clothing. In today's world we can finally appreciate the effort and skill it must have taken to make the embroideries we cherish.

It is astounding that so much has been preserved. Almost any household with any record of geographical stability boasts some inherited needlework. And an unenlightened age which decreed that no one be actually married until ''she hath child bearing pillows, ready stitched, and likewise the mantle for the boy is finished'' produced needlework now selling for gigantic sums at auction. That harsh English law also was the beginning of the custom of gathering together all that would be needed for marriage and put into a chest. The blanket chest – then the more recent ''hope chest.'' The hope chest – that very attractive, cedar lined low chest we are now buying with great enthusiasm as an unusual piece of furniture as well as great storage space.

The blanket chest is an authentic piece of early Americana and out of financial reach for most of us. In the United States the hope chests were dutifully and lovingly filled with handwork by older family members. The hope chest, the chest itself, seems to have been the province of the Lane Company, and although made in vast numbers, families tend to keep them and so they are not for sale as often as one would wish. They are functional, welcome pieces in any home and more and more are being passed on within the family.

But the hope chest betokened a way of life that was very different, women still had the time to sit and ply their needles, a more leisurely time. My own grandmother was constantly exercising her creativity, working always without patterns. Her quilts, pillow cases and sheet edgings, her hand sewn silks, are legendary in the family and are testimony in large part to the careful ways of the girl for whom they were intended, as well as her own talent. Such is the nature of the hope chest and the things that went into it.

Many of the women of that generation were multi-talented. They performed all the necessary tasks for making a home and family comfortable. They did chores we would disdain. They attended to the niceties of life and they rarely complained. Much of their needlework was necessary, certainly through the 1930s much was the product of the American work ethic about idle hands. The devil simply couldn't pry his way into their busy lives, they couldn't make time for him. That's why so many aprons, or dresses, or nightwear are so incredibly beautiful. Those women cared about what they were doing.

We are busy today, but in different ways, so we have come to a greater appreciation of the work which has gone *before*. We are essentially the preservationist generation and seeking the needlework that kept Grandma so busy is part of our desire to maintain a continuity, a sense of belonging. We collect it not only because it is so lovely, but to prove we are part of a long tradition.

Many of the small things we treasure today seem somewhat trivial, what after all is a little doily – a rather insignificant trifle in the scheme of things – what that doily is in fact is a minor art form, and a tribute to good housekeeping in the early 20th century. An "elegancy" of life if you will.

Now with formica tops on tables and counters, with polyurethane with its soil resistant finishes and with so little time to make or launder them, the doilies seem an anachronism.

Collectors seize on such a situation, collectors realize the potential in these charming tidbits and collectors admire them and want to preserve them, even more interesting collectors want to display them and use them in ususual ways. It is not always the inherent worth of this handmade doily which renders it valuable, although that is a plus. It is what the little scrap represents, the nostalgia, the feelings it engenders. Many younger collectors today are really "hooked" on embroidery.

The dictionary puts it simply "ornamented with designs in needlework, to exaggerate, to embelish. The embelishments are what interest us most often, the personal touches women gave to their stitchery, the decorations they wrought on their clothing and their linens for the home. Embroidery is one of the oldest needlework arts – it was done on some scale by women in every possible economic and social condition, and in almost every case interprets the culture as they knew it.

American embroidery has always been done in a less elaborate way. The urge in this country has always been to simplify and although we have embroideries which seem ornate to us now, most do not mimic the complicated, even magnificently ostentatious European and Eastern examples.

All workers in any craft have their own vocabulary. Embroiderers who so often banded together to improve the art certainly have theirs. The American Indians practiced what we now call "porcupine-quill" embroidery. They also did elaborate and beautiful bead work and both of these are now in the realm of expensive fine art.

Early American "stump work" and the pictures executed with the needle are legacies we cherish and the work so exemplary the names of some of the best of the needleworkers have come down to us and are recognized as superb craftswomen. The Colonial American was delighted to sport embroidered stockings, or stunning waistcoats, books of the day talk of "rosettes embroidered around the hem" or "the edging on the neckline of the round dress." The pictures were done so well and so graphically illustrate the scene they have long been the province of museums and are never likely to come our way. Of course, never is a dangerous word in the collecting field. Imagine finding something like that which we could afford.

All the needlework of that period, the crewel, the endless (thank heaven) quilting are testimony to the elegance of mind of even the most humble stitcher. It really tells the story of Colonial America.

One of the sleepers of some years ago were the hooked rugs – not many people were aware of them. Today try looking for the Victorian examples, something affordable and charming. Look at things more recent – I own several from the country's centennial in 1976, which I bought for very little. Certainly a collectible already. In the meantime, as with all needlework, a delightful thing to own.

Contemporary embroidery is being done on a large scale, the stitchers are really reviving the craft in a slightly different way and one of the most popular with them is the needlepoint picture which adorns many a home today. Marvelously decorative and often done from its. Not quite the Bayeaux tapestry but pleasant for the home and very easy on the eye.

The Victorians in their sentimental way were very fond of biblical scenes and many of their needlework pictures are taken right from the Bible. The sense they had of covering things with other things accounts for much of the really gorgeous needlework that survives in their chair seats and backs. All the magazines of the day, and there were many, were chock full of things for ladies to embroider – antimacassars, bags of all sorts including the handbag of the day – the reticule – cushions, pillow cases, runners, tablecloths, bedspreads, clothes, cases, anything you can think of the Victorians had a cover it which is wonderful for us.

But what the early Victorians excelled in during the 1850s was Berlin work which was done on a canvas backing. The colors were extremely bright and seem not to have faded at all and the technique was relatively simple. The best of this work has been collected and for some years since it is so attractive. What the collector should seek are some smaller, less important items, such as the bookmarks. A collection of these can be marvelous, each can be a gem with its individual embroidered exhortation, or the name and date of the maker.

In the 1920s and 1930s era, try for the small handbags which often show exquisite workmanship and design. Try for some of the pillows which sometimes have the maker's initials in the corner – they too are most likely to show superior skill in execution. The important thing is to look and keep looking.

Recently I bought a pair of needlepoint bedroom slippers, the embroidery very well done. The dealer knew nothing about them but obviously they were '20s or '30s work. Embroidery was on anything and everything, much of it can still be bought if we are willing to collect from the later periods.

Embroidery has never gone out of style – it is ancient and on-going. It certainly must have filled creative needs of the maker, now it is filling the needs we have as collectors.

Care

Good sense prevails when caring for your embroideries. The laundering or cleaning depends on the basic materials and the kinds of threads used. Some of the old recipes for laundering are interesting.

In 1920 women were advised to whiten a centerpiece which had become yellowed by soaking the article in buttermilk, then washing in the usual way. A few years earlier it was suggested that tatted work be soaked in soap and water "using a good white soap. Then scrub it with a toothbrush, boil and rinse in bluing water, dip it in borax water, spread it on a clean white paper and brush it out into perfect shape with a toothbrush until dry. When almost dry press it on the wrong side and it will look almost as good as new."

Another – "When laundering an embroidered linen doily or centerpiece for the first time it usually puckers in the center. To avoid this dip the plain center in thin boiled starch holding the embroidered edges in the hand so they do not get wet. Dry again, then dampen well before pressing and it will press out smooth."

Some of this is excellent advice, although now we may safely substitute a mild or soapless detergent for fine pieces and a spray starch. The toothbrush, the white paper for drying are still valid but it is well to remember the embroideries were used regularly in their day and have survived very well with careful handling. With the good cleaning preparations we have today your treasures should not come to any harm if care and patience are exercised.

LACE

The making of lace was probably first inspired by the beauty and fragility of a spider web. As with most of the stunning things mankind has created, the beginnings were no doubt accidental. A long-ago needlewoman dreaming in the sun, watching a spider spin his web and translating the elegance, the airiness to thought, then to actuality. The practical beginnings of lace making are lost in antiquity which lends an aura to the mystery which is lace.

The word lace is Latin and means "noose," a rather grim derivation for something always thought of in terms of refinement and grace. Since lace is basically many strands of thread pulled together to form a design the origin of the word does have a logical connection. There are those who feel it was the fisherfolk of old who saw the need to draw cords or ropes together to form nets which led eventually to fine lace.

Some of the earliest known lace, a primitive type to be sure, has been found in Egypt, and some form of netting has been found among early civilizations, but the early Chinese culture shows no evidence of lace making.

Lace has such a hold on the imagination that countless books and articles have been written about it – definitive, boundless research material is available for lace lovers. The collector should remember that hand made lace is done entirely by the maker, the type and quality results entirely from the originator, but the general category properly includes all openwork weaves which are crocheted, knitted and tatted.

Needlepoint lace is made from a pattern drawn on parchment or dark paper, sewn on linen which makes it easier to separate later. Threads are sewn along the edges to allow the rows of stitches to flowers or leaves or other motifs. When all is finished the stitches fastening the outline cord to the linen are cutaway and voila – lace. Bobbin lace is sometimes so fine one would think the wee people had been at work. Sometimes it is made with silver, gold or silk. These wondrous threads are wound on bobbins. The pattern drawing is attached to a pillow (pillow lace) or cushion and the pins are pushed partially into the drawing. The visible parts of the pins form the framework which the worker builds up into the lace itself. As each part is finished the pins are removed and replaced into the repeat part of the design.

21

When linen began to be used for outer clothing in the 15th century the possibilities for lace use dramatically increased. Paintings of that era portray both kinds of lace and art is a good source of viewing the lace of earlier times. Much of the really old lace is convent lace, and ecclesiastical garments were often lavishly decorated with it.

"Punto in aria" seems an apt description of lace making – literally "out of nothing," a term applied to Point lace which altered the fashion and economic life of Europe. Although they did not go out to work in our sense of the word, many women in Europe earned a decent livelihood making lace. The demand was so great, and the amount of money spent on it so huge, laws were passed to curtail it use – the "Sumptuary Laws."

Nothing rivals the 17th century lace made in France. France under Louis XIV was the apex of the lace making period. The extravagant use of lace with so much money being spent to acquire it, with the dandies and ladies of the court parading in laces costing a fortune and finally even that great spender himself, Louis, passed laws limiting its use on clothing. Ironically, while he as a politician inveighed against this costly luxury, the King as a lover of luxury himself was busily fostering lace making and draping himself in it. Everyone ignored the edict anyway. Everyone of every class tried to own and wear a little lace and eventually the discontent of the populace over this and other manifestations of corruption led to the bloody revolution. It was Louis' minister Colbert though who saw the future for French laces and it is to him we owe the marvelous, incredible 17th century French laces which are so valuable today.

Lace is unique. What is it after all? Held in the hand it seems a beautiful nothing, almost like holding patterned air, but much has occurred in history in its name. It probably figures in more painting and other artwork than any other single artifact, first appearing in an early Florentine picture. There is evidence that people gambled the lace on their caps and tuckers. Lace has always been a symbol of status, more than for its beauty it was often worn to designate the social place in the sun of the wearer. Since its cost was so high the more lace the more it marked the wearer as a person of wealth and importance. Even now lace has some of this aura, but it is difficult for us to place ourselves in a position of understanding about the wearing of lace – now all clothing in the United States is homogenized – a millionaire wears jeans and a t-shirt and certainly no lace. The role of lace in history is long and involved. Some countries lived and died by it in early Europe.

Only a few samples of the lavish Renaissance lace have survived, it was phased out toward the end of the 18th century and it was obviously beautiful. Needlework is always a reflection of the times, that is an historical judgment from a certain point in time – one writer of the 18th century called needlework one of the "gentle arts" neglecting the fact that many of the most revered, beautifully embroidered tapestries show scenes of bloody battles and other carnage.

There are many designations for types of lace and books detailing definitions exist in profusion. Many names of certain laces reflect their place of origin such as Valenciennes or Rouen. The old, priceless handmade lace is in many cases now considered "national treasure" in many countries and is displayed proudly in national museums, and even early machine made lace is becoming a prized possession. When the earliest machine made lace appeared it presented an enormous threat to the livelihood of many and lace purists felt a sense of doom, but machine made laces can be exquisite and are gaining in value.

Many laces made of silk or linen are now made with cotton and cannot be considered authentic in the sense of lace. There is absolutely no reason though to eschew the machine made laces. As collectors know they are often beautiful and well done and while not so fine certainly they have their own charm. Not everyone can, or wants to, afford the old laces – "lacis" as the Quinton material was called or "Buratto" as it was known in Italy. The price of these laces is prohibitive and if a small piece can be acquired for a collection, consider yourself lucky. Many shops are now devoted to selling small pieces of rare laces.

Lace life changed with the Victorians. They were, as usual, very busy making lace but the period was traumatic for all industry. Lace making, which was essentially a "cottage industry" was affected by the change. The reason we cherish hand made lace, aside from it fairy like beauty, is the fact that skilled hands, most of them in their own cottages, made every inch of it with love and care. Nothing made by machine can ever evoke the feeling present when a collector holds something made by a specific person in the past.

Because "what is lovely never dies" as Thomas Bailey said, we still covet lace. So the Victorians in their customary fashion got on with it and continued to make lace, by machine it is true, but lace which we appreciate today.

Recently I had occasion to speak at a seminar on the subject of early American samplers. During the question period we wandered into a discussion of fabrics. Since this audience was not directly concerned with lace I was surprised with a query regarding the "sense" of collecting small piece of lace. Although I responded politely, only later did the perfect response occur to me. John Ruskin said it and I now have it well imprinted in my memory for future snappy comebacks. "Remember the most beautiful things in the world are the most useless; peacocks and lilies, for example." In truth, lace even in small segments can be useful, and it seems fortunate that so many new collectors appreciate it.

The Victorians did not number among the philistines. Although handmade lace was dying out as a lucrative hand craft, machine made laces were gaining a bigger audience even though most women in the Victorian period (and some of this lingers today) had the attitude that only foreign lace added that needed distinction. Lace of the Victorian period, made by machine for the most part, is now being widely sought after and it is encouraging to hear of museum showings and that large private collections are being built.

There are those who will choose only the best and of course that is wonderful for future generations as well as for the collector if the purse permits and that is your primary interest. There are others who tend to admire the small imperfections of the home craftswomen whose mistakes always trigger speculation of who she was, what was she thinking about?

Before cotton came into wider use about the middle of the 19th century and gradually replaced linen, lace was expensive. But cotton lace, made by machine sometimes to very exacting standards was often unexpectedly splendid. Copies of Valenciennes, or Mechlin (so favored by the dandies of the Regency period) can be impressive. One has only to look at a table set with a Quaker Company machine-made cotton lace tablecloth to realize how outstanding this lace can sometimes be. The Quaker Lace Company, after some pre-history was incorporated in 1911, and in 1932 its first Nottingham lace tablecloth was designed. Nineteen thirty-two was the depth of the depression, Quaker Lace was immediately popular, the company prospered and has passed into the realm of Americana, a name we grew up with, a name still famous for quality and integrity and most important to us collectors, probably did more to promote machine made lace than anyone else. The company still used the old Nottingham machines, still an American company in

24

an oasis of foreign ownership.

It's amazing how lace has made a comeback. The old hand-made lace is difficult to care for, but if the collector opts for smaller samples there are ingenious ways to frame them for hanging.

Lace is still available at special sales, auctions and collectors are beginning to communicate with each other for trading. French lace continues to be the most desirable and highest priced but there is much that was exported from Belgium, Ireland and England during the Victorian years. England did a thriving business exporting as well as importing.

Collectors find the acquisition of hand-made lace gratifying not only for what it is but for its history. Research is fairly easy since so much has been written about it and since most books are profusely illustrated. The Victorians were in love with lace and needlework in general so they too filled the shelves with books about the subject. Old catalogues are a tremendous source of identification and museums are slowly making research tools available.

Most large museums, including the Metropolitan Museum of Art in New York are repositories of magnificent laces but if you intend to view it make an appointment well in advance. By all means take advantage of every facility you can when engrossed in the study of lace. The Smithsonian Institution and the Chicago Art Museum also have representative collections.

The popularity of lace has waxed and waned over the centuries and the United States came very late to the manufacturing of it. This country was one of the prime markets for foreign exporters for a long time.

With the advent of lace making machines, the classic hand made laces for all practical purposes disappeared. From our vantage point it's interesting to view the opinions of our forebearers about lace. The German laces, for example, the laces of Germany of the late 1800s were not considered "important laces" by many publications devoted to the art of lace or by lace sophisticates, although German trade was considerable and its main market in 1900 was the United States. Many Germans had settled here and were attracted to the wares of the homeland. A very fertile hunting ground for collectors.

Almost all countries boasted some lace making. Some were particularly fine and recently I purchased some in Killarney. Many pieces have descended in families and are in excellent condition. Any lace which is collected today which has a provenance has added value.

Today there is a resurgence in the collecting, using and wearing of embroidery, lace and old linens. In this country an amazing number of things of great beauty were made in the 1920s, 30s and the early 40s. Now we have come to recognize their value and are attempting to save the best of it. Less than the best has its own charm and should not necessarily be neglected, it is all a paen of praise to those who tried their best and often achieved more than that.

Lace is romantic and ethereal and this impression is reinforced by the fact that many Victorian laces (Chantilly lace, too) were black. An interesting aspect of lace collecting is trying to identify the "occasion" lace – the bridal lace, the pillow lace, the christening lace, the cravat lace – as well as the towns and cities from which much lace originated. The Italian lace has romantic names and Italy did export much lovely lace. It is advisable to track down older relatives to see if they have preserved any laces from their years in another country.

The Cooper-Hewitt Museum recently held a showing of lace and in staging exhibits of this type proves that lace is making a big comeback. There is a growing feeling that lace should be showcased as an art form. The ancient laces are magnificent, no doubt of that but we are concerned here with 19th and 20th century laces and linens which suit our needs and our pocketbooks as well as our aesthetic sense, fit our decorating ideas and do not disrupt our budget.

It is the small touches which give a room character and personalize it. Small needlework objects give just such a finish. Decorators have always recognized this precept. Things that are useable, portable and/or collectible. Our decorating ideas are changing somewhat. We are moving well away from the clinical look and the plethora of magazines devoted to such subjects proves we are trying to personalize our homes, put our "stamp" on them. Needlework in almost any form does this admirably. Even the Vanderbilts and Astors knew that. With their immense fortunes they collected expensive laces and that eclectic collector J. Pierpont Morgan spent fabulous sums for old embroidery.

Someday, some collector reading this book will be remembered in the same way. "Mrs. Smith, that definitive collector of 20th century lace, will make an appearance at the town hall on Saturday, April 7th," the notice will read. Are you that Mrs. Smith?

Care

Caution is the watchword when dealing with lace. Old lace is particularly fragile and although it often needs cleaning when found, it should be washed by hand with great care. Some collectors recommend distilled water and the mildest detergent. Others feel tap water is suitable when used with a soapless detergent. Ideas for safe laundering abound, all agree that patience and care are necessary. There are those who think that placing large lace articles in a mesh bag makes handling easier. Others have mentioned that putting a large piece, a lace tablecloth for instance, in the bathtub between sections of netting half filling the tub with lukewarm water and a soapless detergent, leaving it for about 10 minutes while gently swishing the water and raising and lowering the top net piece, will do the trick. Some laces will shrink so always be careful about water temperature; and place the lace on an entirely smooth surface for drying.

Repairs to old lace are the province of a professional unless you are highly skilled yourself. Contact the local museum textile curator for advice if you own some valuable heirloom, otherwise sensible, careful washing and drying – no harsh abrasive liquids or soaps, and patience should be adequate. Try to keep your lace out of the way of dust if possible although your lace should always be displayed where one can appreciate its great beauty.

Wear it, frame it, lay it out in drawers which can sometimes be used as display for visitors; if it is essential to put it away always use acid-free tissue paper to wrap it.

I have found my Great Grandmother's advice is wonderful and works well. As she was removing things from an old trunk one day she unwrapped an old linen tablecloth, soft and pliable with age and use. In it lay her lace wedding veil in almost pristine condition. When I remarked on this she said, ''It's something I was told many years ago, it's the old linen, it keeps the veil clean and lets it breathe.'' I never forgot that image, the lace veil busily breathing. It's true though. Try wrapping your old lace in old linen. For this purpose I now save or buy any old soft linen in which to cosset my old lace.

Anything worth buying and keeping is worth caring for. So it certainly is with old lace. Lace is luxury, lace is practical; lace is elegant, lace can edge an apron; lace is everyday, lace is high fashion. Lace is beautiful, lace is an investment.

Lace is becoming all things to all collectors. Take care of it.

Machine Made Lace

During the 1920s and 30s machine made lace had a tremendous impact on fashion as well as the fabric business. Lace was seen on everything and companies of every size flourished. It seems almost impossible to protect individual designs in lace although many companies tried. Nevertheless patents offered minimum protection since with the slightest variation lace could be renamed and sold as an original design.

Those unsung heroes, the designers were hard at work. Week after week many design applications were filed for protection on their ideas.

In the early 1920s there were dozens of companies, large and small, vying for the lace trade. The lace itself could be made and sold fairly cheaply but behind all the brisk buying and selling were the designers. Unlike the old handmade product where a woman could sit and design as she went, the machines required programming and the programmers were the designers.

Whenever you, the collector, handle a piece of lace, think of the mind which created it, be it hand made or machine made. It first had to be a thought in someone's mind. The piece you are holding required inventiveness and imagination before the process of manufacture could begin.

Typical laces and embroideries of the 1920s-1930s period and their designers prove that a machine in those days was only as good as the person who dealt with it. Studying these examples will give the collector new insight into the creative work going on at that time in the field of lace.

Machine made lace often shows superior design work and of course the machine itself guaranteed that the finished product would look good. Not old Chantilly perhaps, but in its own way and placed properly in time, a thing to collect, appreciate and love.

The following four pages show a small sampling of machine made lace.

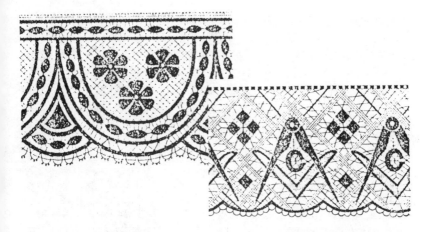

Left: The American Fabrics Co., a Connecticut corporation, manufactured this lovely lace in the early 1920s. It was designed by Samuel H. Page of Stamford, Conn. Right: Samuel H. Page was a prolific designer in the early 1920s. Most of his designs were made by the American Fabrics Co. of Connecticut. This specialty lace features the Masonic symbol.

These three designs are by Samuel H. Page for the American Fabrics Co., Connecticut. 1920-1925.

Some interesting design work by Henry Schwarber of Weehawken, N.J. done in 1930. These were all intended as edgings.

Embroidered lace collar by Alexander N. Hirth for the W.S. Embroidery Works, Inc. of Cliffside Park, New Jersey. The wearing of machine made lace collars was an almost necessary fashion accessory for women in the 1930s in order to refurbish old clothing. This was designed in 1930.

Designs for an embroidered textile fabric by Ernest W. Freudenberg of Amrein Freudenberg Co. of New York. As with many smaller companies of all kinds in the 1920s and 30s the owner was also the designer of the products. 1932.

Right: The quality of this machine made lace is often outstanding as evidenced here in this design of Lawrence Dinkelspiel of West New York, N.J. and Edwin Bosshardt of Hudson Heights, N.J. for their own company - Harnapp, Dinkelspiel & Co., Inc. of New York. 1923.

Thomas Monk was another designer who produced many beautiful patterns. These wide laces were created in the early 1920s and show great delicacy.

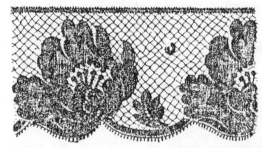

Left: Hans Albert Philips designed this lace pattern for American Fabrics Company of Connecticut in the early 1920s.

Right: This doily, centerpiece or scarf or 'similar article' was the work of Hans Albert Philips for the American Fabrics Co. of Conn. 1921.

Left: Samuel H. Page designed this one for American Fabrics Co. of Connecticut in the period 1920-1925.

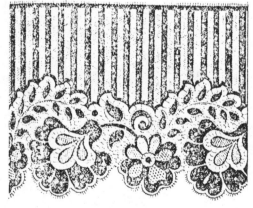

Right: Connecticut Lace Works of Norwalk Connecticut produced this fine design by Thomas Monk of Bridgeport, Con.. It was made in 1921.

Collars and collar and cuff sets have always been sought after. They not only lend themselves to a collection of needlework because of their variety and the fact that they can be easily framed or displayed but because they are a wearable collectible. The top collar is from the 1930's and is of ecru linen with cutwork, beautifully embroidered flowers and hand sewn, attached machine lace. Value $25-45

The center collar is very heavy ecru crochet from a child's summer coat. 5'' wide. Value $35-45

The interesting collar on the bottom of photograph was worn on a beige print dress before 1920. Value $35-45

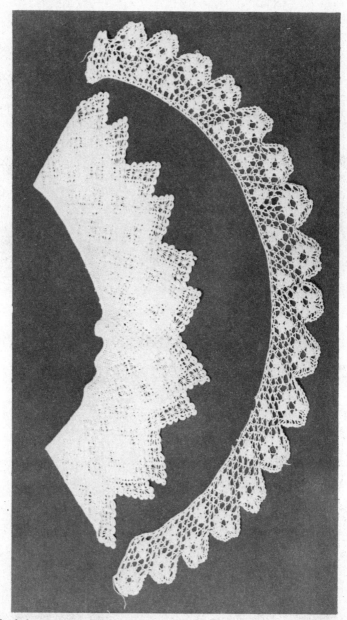

At left of photograph is one of a pair of 8'' magnificently crocheted edgings intended for pillowcases but obviously never used for that purpose. These could be used in other ways without damaging the original intent.

Pair, value $50-85

Right is a collar of rather ordinary design but well done as most of the surviving pieces are.

Value $30-40

A magnificent collar. The lace collector competes with the Vintage Clothing collector when quality collars and cuffs are involved. The leaves here are filled with herringbone or cross-stitch, single and double and the webs - point d'Alencon.

Value $75-100

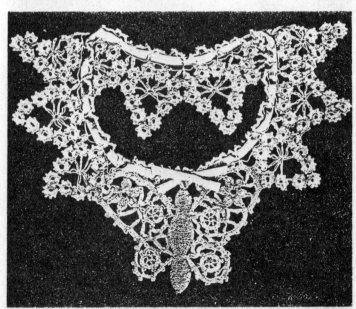

This collar is a gem. This kind of fancy work is in great demand. It shows imagination in design and excellence of execution. A beautiful addition to a collection.

Value $75-95

This wide, pointed collar has a sleeve edging which gives it a nice neat finish. The satin ribbon, threaded through, is a delicate touch to a rather overall heavy look. The workmanship cannot be faulted though.   Value $50-60

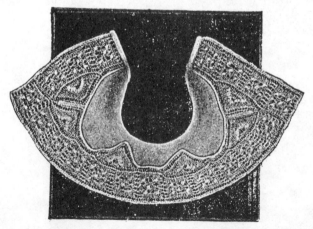

Although examples of good knit work can be exquisite there are not many collectors who specialize in this kind of needlework. Here is a lovely collar in pink knit with very wide edging. It complements the pink organdy by its subtle shading. This was made about 1923 or 1924.   Value $35-45

This is a lovely, delicate collar, useful and beautiful. Collars of this quality are much sought after and are rising in price.   Value $55-75

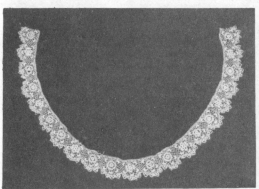

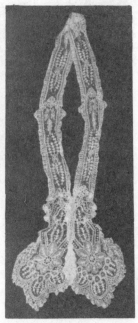

The dainty lace collars are among the most sought after of all the older pieces. These are highly decorative and fit in well with today's fashions. The hand crocheted collar on the right is only 1½'' wide.
Value left $50-65
Value right $45-55

A delightful bow knot adorns this crocheted yoke. All these yokes, while made for the same purpose of being part of another garment, can be found in an amazing range of shapes and patterns. Since most were made by women at home the quality can be uneven but even when less than perfect they can be a good addition to a collection.

Value $50-55

All of these pieces are of exquisite workmanship. They are part of a large legacy of handmade collars and cuffs, and all of them are currently in use on contemporary clothing. The top one is one of a pair of cuffs, one end showing the eyes which accept the hooks which are covered and not visible.   Value of pair $60-75

The center collar is quite spectacular, more than 6'' wide in ecru color. The imaginative design work is evident as is the skill of the maker.   Value $75-100

The longer collar on bottom is notable not only for its length but for its perfect proportions. Ecru.   Value $70-80

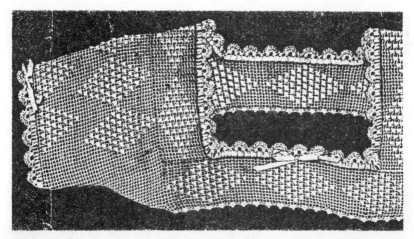

This crocheted yoke with sleeves has a more everyday look than some of the intricate floral and figural designs. The skill of the needlewoman is evident and a fairly large collection could be made of just such yokes.   Value $65-85

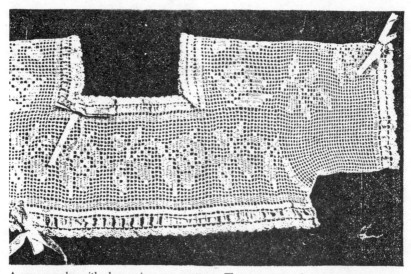

A square yoke with sleeves in a rose pattern. These square yokes were enormously popular in the early years of the century and well into the 1930's. They reflect good design and workmanship and were usually added to garments of fine materials.
Value $75-95

21'' tatted collar, ecru. 4'' wide, 10 medallions. Early 1900's.   Value $40-45

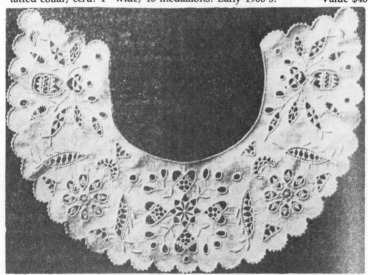

In 1906 when all kinds of white open embroidery was so much in demand this collar is an example of Danish cut-work or Hedebo (Hay-the-bow) embroidery, one of the types. While not too difficult it is nevertheless an exacting skill. All the designs of Danish cut-work are formed of geometrical figures such as hearts, diamonds, ovals or circles. Usually sprays of small oval leaves, or simple wreaths are worked in satin stitch and placed around and between the cut-work groups. This is an elaborate collar. Value $40-50

41

A fine scalloped yoke in crochet. 1916. These are usually found in good condition and ready to wear on a favorite dress or to be framed or otherwise displayed as part of a needlework collection.   Value $65-85

Left: Collar and cuffs of Cluny lace which gave a dainty look which women were seeking in the early 1900s.   Value $150-175
                                                                                 Value $250-275

Center: In the period 1900-1910 Cluny lace was at the height of its popularity and was much used for all sorts of neck and sleeve insertions. Here are two examples.
                                                                                 Value $150-175

Right: The star effect in this Cluny lace collar was destined to dress up a plain frock.
                                                                                 Value $125-150

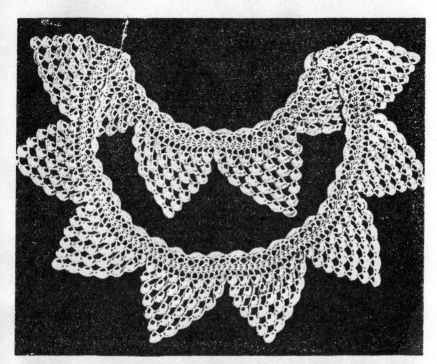

This yoke has a heavier look than some of the others shown, but it shows the care and skill with which women worked on these pieces. Often this work was done as a way to keep oneself busy in what was then considered a purely feminine way. Many of these yokes and collars can be found today on exquisite nightwear of the period.

Value $55-60

A very good illustration of the jabot. The jabot at left is in two parts, the smaller to be placed over the larger and attached at the top, the bows are embroidered, buttonholed on the edges and the openings whipped over and over as eyelets for velvet ribbon to be run through. The jabot at the right is embroidered to simulate plaits, the lines simply outlined and the flowers in solid colors.

Value $30-40
each

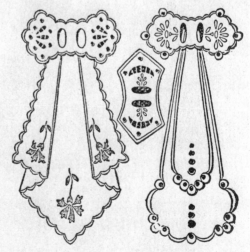

Coat set in Irish crochet c. 1900. The motifs used in this set are few and fairly simple yet the whole is pleasing and most effective. This is due partly to the variety of filling stitches and the very well done daisy design. The shapes of both collar and cuffs are also attractive.   Value $100-150

44

The motifs for this collar were made separately and basted onto the cambric pattern, then filling stitches were put in. This collar has many motifs which lend interest not only to the wearer but probably to the maker. Made in 1914.

Value $45-65

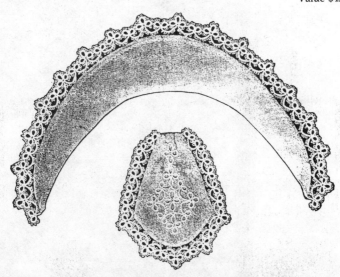

The simple tatted edging on this collar and jabot, while not spectacular, is nicely done. It is difficult to find such a set and today we do not often recognize the jabot by its correct name although it was a popular fashion well into the 1930's. This is from 1914.

Value $40-50

Duchess and Renaissance lace bertha collar (23"x23"), yoke 12"x13" and cuffs for elbow sleeves 13"x3½". This set is very artistic and was made in 1901 when hand made lace was much in vogue. The time and skill necessary to make such a set rendered it unique and so utterly fashionable. A labor of love.

Value $145-175

A stunning collar and revers originally worn on a jacket. Russian lace. The braid is cream colored. 1901.

Value $100-135

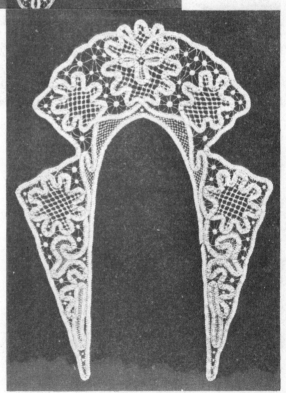

Yoke of French Cluny braid - front and back. Worked design. Graceful form with its flowing scroll design and elaborate stitchery. Cream braids and thread. 1901.

Value $95-145

A dainty chiffon handkerchief with a wide lace border. Light blue. Embroidered flowers with french knots. Hankies are now a developing collecting field and represent a wide range of materials, trims and quality. This is particularly pretty. Many fine handkerchiefs are overlooked and underpriced.   Value $10-20

The wide lace border of this linen wedding handkerchief is attached with stitches so fine as to be invisible. c. 1900.   Value $38-48

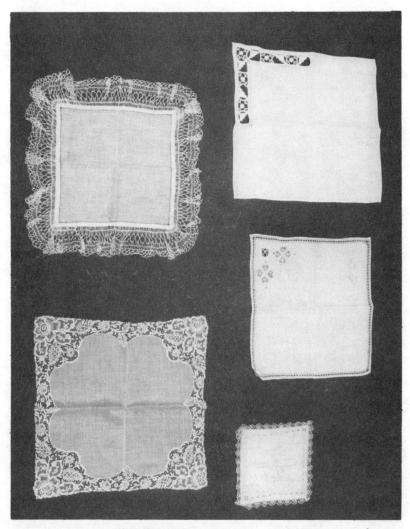

A selection of handkerchiefs of varying sizes and decoration. It is amazing what one can find in the handkerchief collecting field at very little cost. These are all lovely, with the right three rather plain but still skillfully finished and cornered. The top left is a wedding hankie, most valued of all.

Left, each $30-50
Right, each $10-20

Top L-R: Cotton batiste handkerchief, cut work corner, tatted edging. Value $30-45
An 1890's wedding handkerchief of silk. These exquisite hankies are often found in
pristine condition, having been carried only once.   Value $30-45
Bottom L-R: Cotton napkin. Floral design with bow in corner, scalloped edge. Set of 12.
                                                                    Value $85-95
Lawn handkerchief, very fine, tiny flowers in the lace edging.   Value $25-35

In the last several years handkerchiefs of all types have acquired many new dedicated collectors. The type shown here is in a class by itself, considerably more valuable than the dated or subject or art type. This hankie is of linen with Torchon lace and with insertions. Many collectors of handkerchiefs tend to frame them.   Value $30-35

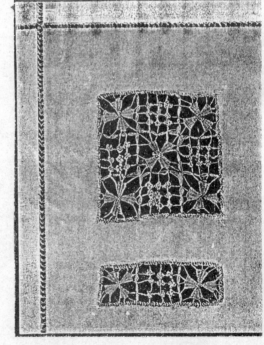

Linen handkerchief showing corner detail. The sense of rigidity evident in machine made decoration is completely absent.   Value $20-30

A gorgeous Point Lace handkerchief. Cambric. Value $35-45

Another exquisite handkerchief in Point Lace. The stitches here are primarily Sorrento bars and wheels, and Point Lace fillings. The leaves of the corner flowers are filled with point de Tulle, point de Sorrento and point de Valenciennes; the border leaves with point de Venice and point de Sorrento. All extremely popular laces. Value $40-60

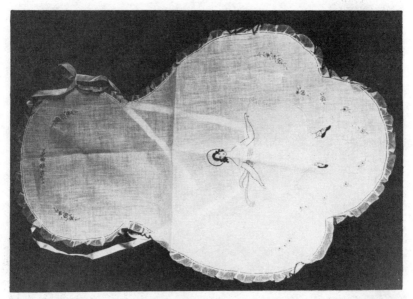

A delightful organdy apron. Yellow ribbon straps cross in back. Black haired ballerina wears yellow costume and black slippers. Machine lace trim.   Value $25-28

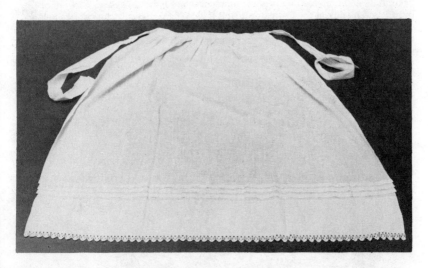

Aprons often show a surprising attention to detail and many times are exquisite examples of stitchery. As a collectible the apron is still undervalued and under-appreciated. This apron which tied at the waist is a 'half apron' in white cotton with 1½'' crocheted edging. The length of these aprons was usually about 36 inches. c. 1900.
                                                            Value $40-50

Floor length apron, Egyptian cotton with plaid weave. Wide sash ties and bottom flounce beautifully embroidered. Vintage clothing collectors have always been aware of the beauty and quality of the lowly apron and it is to them that collectors of needlework owe a hearty thank you. The apron is an underestimated collectible which is both interesting and often quite handsome. This dates from the 1880's and is in perfect condition.
Value $100-150

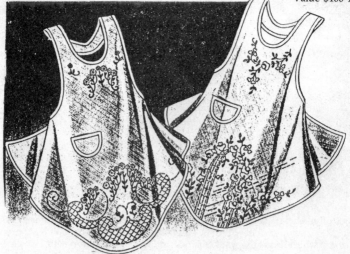

Often overlooked in the quest for good embroidery examples are the everyday aprons of the 1930's. The two shown here are fast color chambray, neatly bound and intended for ample dress protection. The stamped designs are nicely embroidered. These can be found in bright colors.
Value $25-35

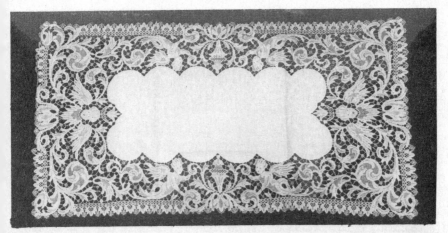

Above: This scarf with its fine linen center is, aside from its beauty, a genuine conversation piece with its angels so clearly visible. Many younger collectors are drawn to this kind of work and prices are going up in proportion to rising interest. It is difficult to find pieces of this quality except in the finest shops.   Value $175-195

White cotton bloomers with white 4'' eyelet ruffles. As examples of fine needlework these early bloomers are often outstanding, as reminders of those bad ''good old days'' they are unique.   Value $95-125

White cotton batiste bloomers with ruffles, edged with machine made lace. Bloomers are now considered museum type memorabilia and collectors of either vintage clothing or needlework are finding it more difficult to compete.   Value $125-195

White cotton split bloomers with drawstring. The bottoms are edged with hand crocheted lace. c. 1890.   Value $125-175

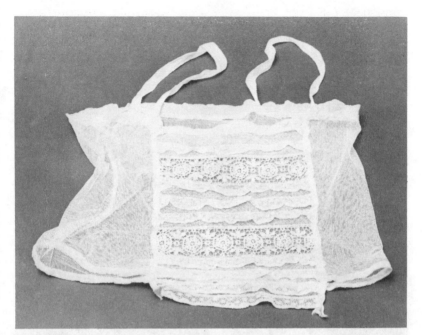

Net gown yoke with lace insertions and trim. Before 1920. White.   Value $55-65

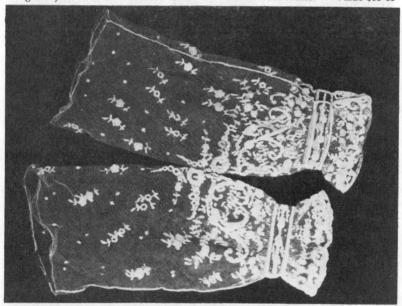

These sleeves were salvaged from a blouse worn in the late 1800s. They have never been resewn on any garment but have been carfully kept, purely for their beauty. Lace has this effect, it is almost never discarded and now is beginning to surface in various guises – either on clothing, still intact or in small snippets kept because of sentimental, esthetic or intrinsic value.   Value $50-65

Left: Beaded bag collections abound but not many people seek out the hand made bags such as are shown here. Not only is this all hand crocheted but each of the 8 section sides is trimmed with embroidery. All lined by hand stitching with colored silk as are the handles. These are a much overlooked collectible, and still way under-priced.   Value $35-45

Right: An unusual knitted work bag. Although not a lady's handbag, these can fit into such a collection as well as into collections of other phases of either needlework or fashion. It is becoming more difficult to find knitted bags of this high quality in good condition. Old rose color, lined with silk and with a square of cardboard at the bottom. This type bag is larger than the ordinary handbag. Quite elaborate. Value $40-60

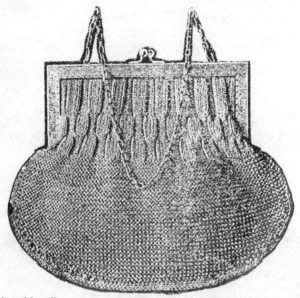

This crocheted handbag, sewn to a metal frame with chain is blue with an old rose silk lining. Sometimes with these bags the lining has to be replaced. Sometimes, too, these bags yield small treasures, recently a tiny gold button was found in one.

Value $35-55

An outstanding knitted handbag in black and gold. The frame would have been bought separately and the knit work sewn to the frame. The bag itself is black and the lining gold silk. When there is more awareness of the beauty and appeal of this type handbag, prices will surely rise.

Value $35-55

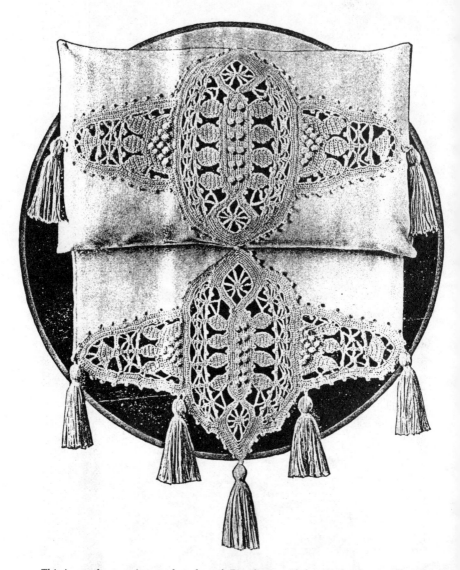

This is a truly stunning crocheted scarf. Ecru linen with heavy tassels magnificently designed and executed crochet work. This is a long scarf emininetly useful and elegant.

Value $100-150

Scarf with trumpet design. As was usual with this kind of work the design was prepared first before the vine embroidery was begun. The centers of the flowers are filled with French knots. The scarf itself is of linen, hemmed, the fringe is then drawn over the hem with a crochet hook. When this is completed, the edging was brushed out and clipped to even the fringe. A striking scarf, and part of a new collecting fetish.

Value $150-200

Left: This is an elaborate tea gown of 1918. Elegantly hand embroidered this at-home dinner gown is of crepe de chine with silk shadow lace. Before so many enthusiastic vintage clothing collectors entered the field, gowns such as this were bought for their laces and trims. In today's collecting climate it would be a rare person who would mutilate such a gown. The 'coatee' is trimmed with filet medallions back and front and elaborately embroidered in silk. The lace is soft and filmy. Ribbon rosette and rosebud.   Value $400-500

Right: In 1913 the Quaker Lace Company was marketing "seasonable patterns of Quaker Lace for the American Woman of Fashion." That year they were advertising their "shadow laces which gave a 'light' effect." These were sold through department stores, dry goods stores and specialty shops. Such high fashion with its lovely lace is a collector's dream.   Value $35-400

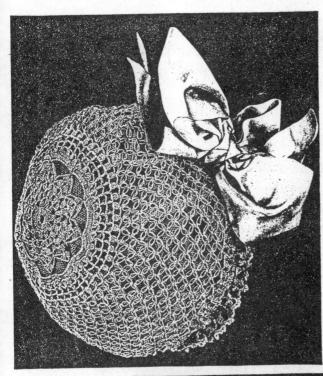

There already exist extensive collections of boudoir caps. They are endearing examples of a fashion which emphasized feminity. The huge satin bow, the lovely medallion and the frothy crochet work make this a prime model of the category.

Value $35-50

This boudoir cap is done in open work, with the medallion, lace edging and wide satin bow, the whole over a net cap. Delightful. Ten years ago caps such as these could be bought for $10 or under, now they have moved into prestigious collections and prices are escalating. Deservedly so.

Value $35-50

The camisole, the chemise and the drawers can be among the most accessible sources of old lace and crochet work. Top L-R: Washable satin camisole trimmed with cream lace in fillet pattern. Straps are of lace. $40-45

Nainsook chemise trimmed with groups of pin tucks, hand embroidered medallions and Valenciennes lace, satin ribbon. Value $45-65

Bottom L-R: Crepe de chine chemise. Valenciennes lace. Blue ribbon. Flap forms a short skirt effect. The chemise is making a minor comeback. Value $45-65

Chemise, nainsook and lace, pin tucks and featherstitching. Value $40-50

The bodices of these nightgowns of the 1915 era show a great attention to materials, handwork and detail. Particularly beguiling to us are the nightcaps which are not only wonderful collectibles but very often things of real beauty. Top left - gown of nainsook, bodice and short sleeves of overall embroidery. Shirring and ribbon drawn. The cap is of Oriental lace trimmed with a double row of satin ribbon.

Top right - Flesh crepe de chine gown with Valenciennes lace forming the yoke back and front, ribbons and rosettes. The cap is of fine ecru net with blue ribbon, ribbon banding and rosettes.

Bottom left - Nainsook gown with bodice of Swiss embroidery. Valenciennes lace trim.

Bottom right - Finest quality nainsook, this gown was made in France. Pin tucks and featherstitching trim. Lace in filet pattern at neck and sleeves. Many pieces of this fine lingerie of this period are marked 'Made in France.'

These nightgowns are another illustration of how the astute collector needs to be alert. Normally the province of the Vintage Clothing collector and dealer, some of the lingerie of the period of the 1920's, 30's and earlier is a source of surprising elegance and skill in the art of needlework. Any of these would be a worthwhile addition to a collection of hand embroidery. The top two are sheer fine nainsook, completely sewn by hand in the Phillipines. The bottom is batiste. Sewn, embroidered and appliqued, every bit hand done. This gown even has a name, it is "genuine Visentita" in honor of a convent nun who designed the work. Anyone of discernment would be interested in acquiring such quality.

Top two, each, $40-50
Bottom $75-95

The Vintage Clothing collector has made serious inroads into the delightful clothing the children wore in earlier times, however, some remarkable examples with hand work can still be had for relatively little money. Any and all such garments are a joy to own and complement any collection of needlework. Typical of dresses worn by toddlers in the early 1930's is the group at top. Left is a white batiste dress with inverted side pleats. Lace edging and embroidered with forget-me-nots and French knot flowers. Center dress is white batiste, hemstitched, lace edgings, hand embroidered and tucked. Right is a white nainsook, hemstitched with lace edging. Fairly simple. Any or all of these would be a choice addition.

Value of dress on left $30-40
center $45-55
right $25-35

Baby dresses are enchanting. Both of these are white nainsook with elaborate hand embroidery.   Each $30-40

67

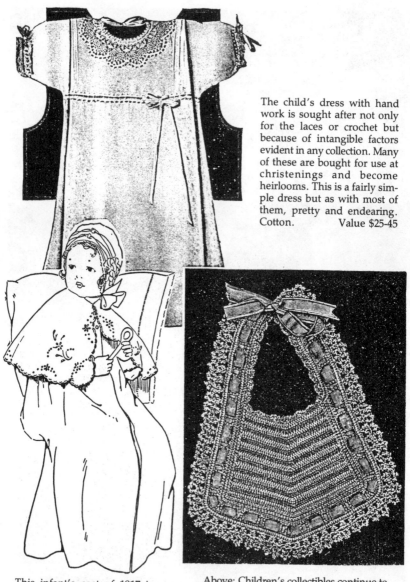

The child's dress with hand work is sought after not only for the laces or crochet but because of intangible factors evident in any collection. Many of these are bought for use at christenings and become heirlooms. This is a fairly simple dress but as with most of them, pretty and endearing. Cotton. Value $25-45

This infant's coat of 1917 is crepe lined with silk, beautifully hand embroidered, the cape and cuffs are hand scalloped. The materials and exquisite hand work render this heirloom coat a valuable acquisition. Value $125-175

Above: Children's collectibles continue to rise in interest. This not only fits into that category but as a piece of needlework it is outstnading. It is a particularly lovely child's bib which incorporates ribbon. An exciting find. Value $45-65

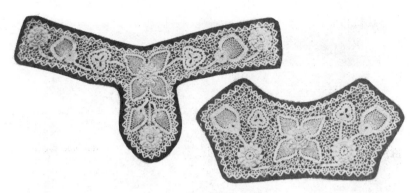

Baby Irish crochet set. This collar and cuff set is executed in the shamrock, rose and thistle design. An heirloom which dates from about 1902.   Value of set $165-185

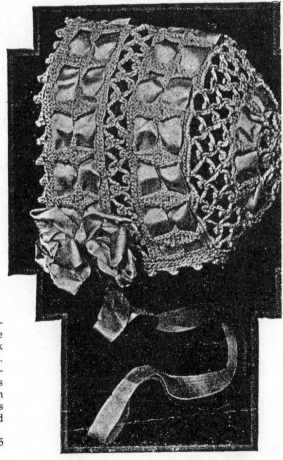

The wide satin ribbons enhance the skilled crochet work on this baby bonnet. A quite typical example of baby caps of the period. I own several large dolls which are dressed with such bonnets.
Value $30-45

Seven separately made wheels are tied together in the center of each touching scallop with knots of ribbon. Although this is a doily, each wheel could be used individually as a drink coaster or 'little doily'.   Value $15-25

A typical doily in the daisy design. These doilies were often used as pincushion covers and a complete set for the dresser was also probable.　　　Doily, value, $7.50-20

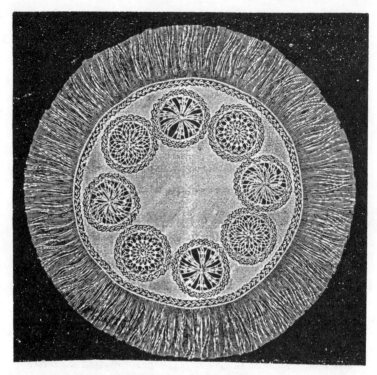

Fringe, so dear to the Victorian heart, is equally enchanting to today's collector. This round doily which is approximately 10 '' without the fringe, was considered "quite new" as a 'drawnwork' technique. The center is linen.   Value $30-45

This doily in the cloverleaf design on fine lawn and with a deep fringe was done with small honiton leaf braid. Very desirable. Value $45-55

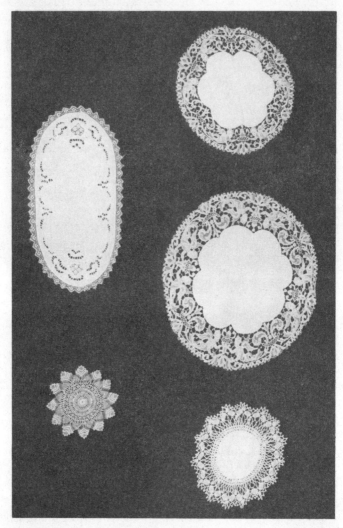

A selection of doilies with lace edgings. Doilies are the most collected of all the needlework pieces. Used in their original way doilies have a cozy quality which seems to add warmth and charm to any home. Taken out of content they can often lend a stunning accent to a room or even on clothing. I have seen them framed, used on pillows, used as handkerchiefs (decorative, of course) used as an insert in an evening skirt, even lightly pasted onto a skylight. Of all the collectible needlework, doilies seem the most nostalgic.

Value of two, bottom left c. 1900, small $45-55, large $55-65
The other three doilies range from $15-35

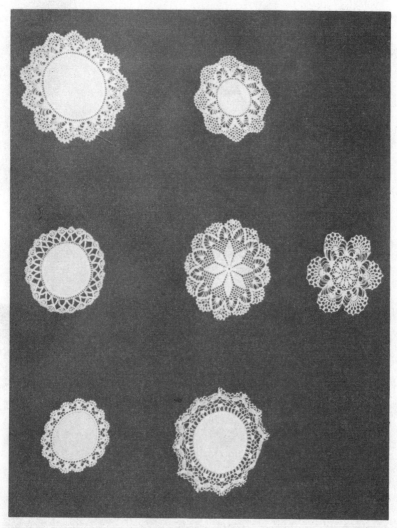

A representative assortment of doilies used under vases, figurines, baskets. Also some individual coasters are pictured. All from the 1920's and '30's and all fine crochet work.

Coasters, each $5-15
Doilies, depending on quality, each $15-35

Doilies, left, ecru crocheted doily, 12"x9". Right: white crocheted doily. c. 1940.
Value $15-25

A typical crochet doily which can be seen in all shops dealing with needlework. These are pretty, fairly common with slight variations and make a good start to a collection.
Value $10-25

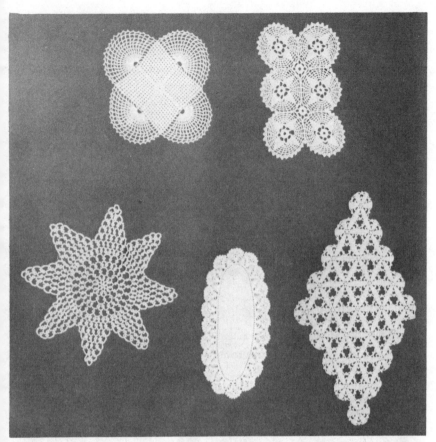

Selection of doilies and an antimacassar. The star shaped doily is tatted, the oval is cotton with crocheted edge, the others are crochet work in different patterns, weight and shapes.   Value of each, $15-30

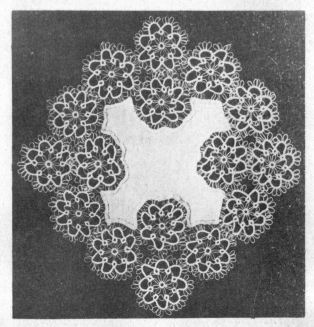

A tatted doily 13''x13'' with linen center, 1899.   Value $55-85

Left: Doily of heavy ecru crochet work, approximately 19'' across, 1930's. Most of the needlework owned by this collector was made by her mother, so it can be dated accurately.   Value $30-35
Right: Pineapple pattern. White crochet, 18''. 1920's. Very desirable pattern.
                                                                 Value $30-35

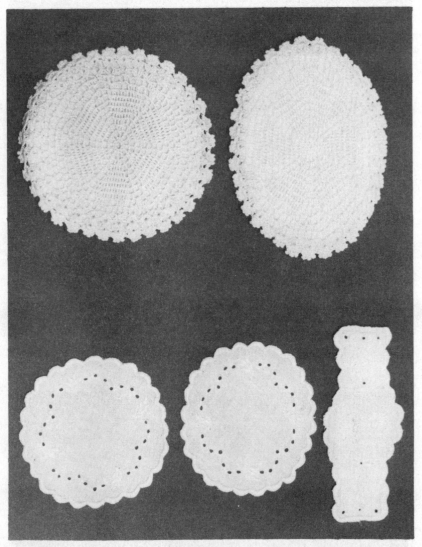

Top: Set of hot pads. Flannel on cardboard inserts are covered by heavy crochet. Made in 1915.　　　　　　　　　　　　　　　　　　　　　　　　Value $15-25

Bottom: Three pieces from a large set of doilies, made in 1912. Cut work linen with scalloped edges. The two top pieces were made to fit under a cream and sugar. There are 10 other doilies of different sizes in the set.　　　　　　Value of set $45-55

Needlework crosses all boundaries and it is often difficult to tell the point of origin. The doily on the left was purchased in Paraguay in the 1960's. It is 14'' round and beautifully delicate. Value $20-25

Right: Linen embroidered white on white. The basket of flowers and embroidered finished edges give this small piece a luxurious air. Value $20-25

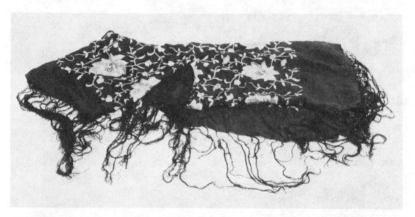

Black silk piano scarf with black silk fringe. Four feet square. Crewel embroidery with shades of gold silk thread. The black silk fringe is 12'' wide. This is rather spectacular and no photograph could do it justice. Value $200-300

Needlework of every description has been employed for table adornment but nothing gives the satisfaction of filmy lace. The centerpiece shown is Flemish lace in the rose and scroll design. Done around 1900.   Value $75-95

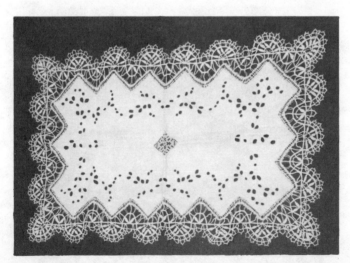

Similar but not an exact match to the larger round cloth in another photo, this scarf was obviously crafted by the same hand. The same level of skill is evident and the same eye for design and proportion. Linen with insert and cut work. Value $65-95

Filet work was enormously popular in the early 1920s. Illustrated here are different edgings for useful items in the home. Left, an unusual edging on a towel; center, the round centerpiece measures 36'' with a basket decoration; the towel on the right has an often-seen edging of crochet and embroidery with slight variations.

Value of towels, each $20-35

A very beautiful Renaissance lace table cover, 30''x30''. Pink cambric.

Value $135-175

Crochet trimmed runner. Cluny, filet and lace stitches are combined in this design. This one was done with natural or unbleached thread on linen exactly matching the color of the thread.   Value $50-70

Nostalgia at its most charming. Filet crochet piano scarf. Often this is not recognized for what it is – even in its heyday it was not found in every home. It is hand made and the shape is distinctive and unusual. 1920.   Value $75-100

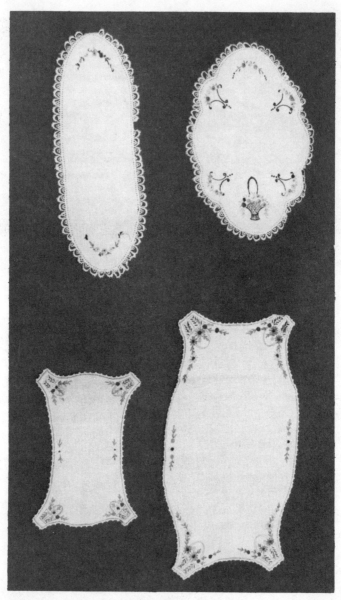

Top: Set of 3 scarves, large center scarf and two smaller ones; cream linen with crocheted edging, embroidered baskets of flowers, French knots, lazy dazy. These were used on dressers which had a center mirror and fold-out side mirrors and on '20's, '30's dressers which had a depressed center and higher sides. Particularly pretty set.
Value $40-50

Bottom: Set for dresser, two small scarves and one longer one. The embroidery is very fine on these, the top one is reversed so the ends of the threads showing.
Value $40-50

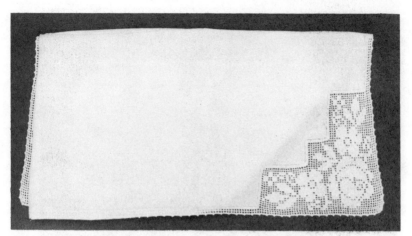

Luncheon cloth, soft linen, beautifully crocheted corners with roses and leaves. Done in the 1920's. 44"x44". Value $35-50

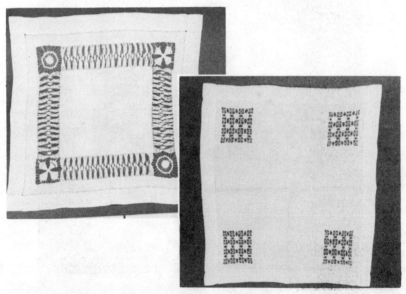

Napkins, both linen. Left: A large, dinner size with drawn work, hemstitched. All hand done. The drawnwork here is especially fine. One of a set of 4. Value of set $50-95
Right: Another large dinner napkin with drawn work corners, hemstitched. One of a set of 4, all hand made. Value of set $50-95

Tea cloth of muslin. Each corner is decorated with a leaf and floral design. Six matching napkins which have the design on only one corner.   Value $45-65

This 23" round 'In-between' cloth is of linen which has become softened through laundering but is nevertheless in perfect condition. The wide crochet border is 3" wide and the whole is a perfect balance. Useful and beautiful.   Value $50-60

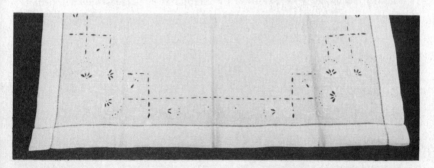

A beautiful white on white luncheon cloth. Linen. The cut work shows here as black spaces. This is a fairly typical cloth except for the very heavy embroidery. Value $45-65

Tea drinking is on the upswing, the tea party is back in vogue, even the Sunday tea dance is waltzing into the social scene. No doubt this accounts for the clamor among collectors for the dainty tea cloth. This one has Old English point with a damask center. A delicate, outstanding collectible which would have been expensive when made.

Value $100-125

One of the charms of these older pieces is their original use; often we do not recognize how or why an interesting embroidered piece was utilized. A good example is the selection of sewing machine covers pictured here. The contemporary scene boasts many home sewers but how many times have you seen a sewing machine covered in this way? These are scarce but are an untapped collecting field and are still mostly unrecognized. Top: One of the endearing types of covers with printed message, "A stitch in Time." Floral and lattice design. Delightful with its lace trim on pure cream linen. Value $45-65

Center: It cannot be emphasized enough that the basket of flowers dominated much embroidery work in the 1930's. Here is another example in this sewing machine cover which is plain on top but trimmed with lace and the quality of the linen evident when laid flat. Value $45-65

Lower: "Sew awhile and be in Style" could be a 1980's TV commercial for one of the large fabric chains. This has the 'lily pond' design on white 'Indian head' with a narrow lace trim. Value $45-65

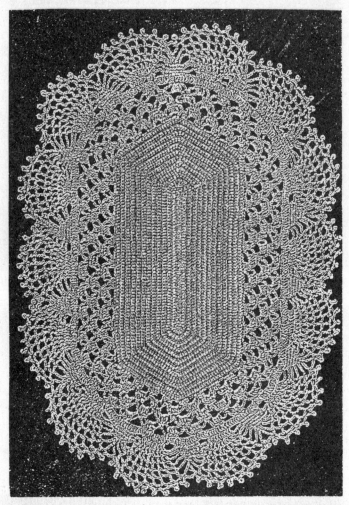

This is a table mat, one of a set of five. As any collector of older linens knows, our forebears were inordinately fond of sets. This is a pretty covering for the table center or dresser, and the workmanship is excellent. This type of set is much in demand now.

Table mat value $45-50

Although collectors of Victoriana tend to see and buy isolated better examples of furniture and the bibelots of the period, the total look was fussy and overdone as this photograph proves. The individual artifacts - the frame, the lamp, the work basket - are all worth our efforts, but it is the table cover (and Victorians were overly fond of table covers) which attracts our attention here, although in the Victorian way it almost obscures the lovely table. The deep fringe on these cloths is still considered very attractive and the embroidery carefully and nicely done.

Value of table cloth $75-85

A pretty tatted centerpiece, linen. The wheels, both large and small are made separately. The linen edges cut in a scallop. Often a paper pattern was used on the linen for accuracy. These small items involved much hand work and time which in this machine age adds so much to their value.   Value $25-40

This tablecloth of linen looks similar to Battenberg but is done differently. A large cloth and worth many times what any collector would pay for it or anything nearly resembling it from the same era.   Value $250-350

Closeup of one corner of a tablecloth. This has great beauty with its designs of twisted bars, spider web wheels and stylized palm leaves. Sometimes this or quite similar designs are found on old curtains. Renaissance lace.　　　Value of cloth $200-250

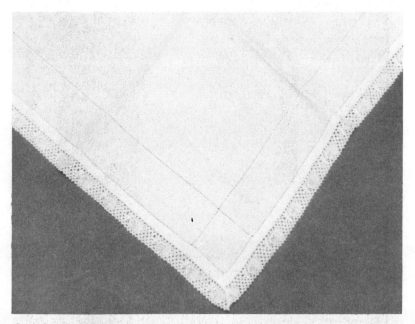

One of a set of four lovely, soft linen napkins. All hand made, the lace edging is ¾" wide, each has an embroidered corner and the stitching so tiny as to be almost invisible. Each napkin is 13"x14". Part of the beauty of these pieces is the time and dedication it took to complete them.   Value of set of 4 napkins $45-55

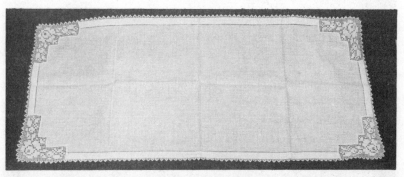

Short table runner, part of a set. Linen, fancy edging, 4 corners crocheted in flower and leaf design.   Value of set, cloth and 4 place mats $45-75

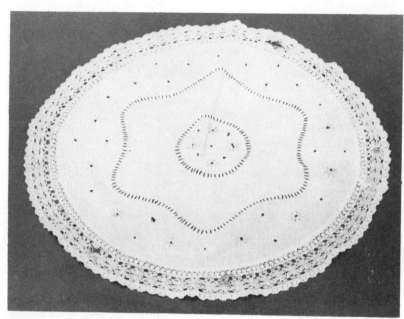

18'' circle centerpiece. White light linen embroidered with pink, yellow and white daisies with black French knots in the centers. Edged with unusual machine made white lace, inserts of pink silk bows. Lace 1½'' wide.   Value $35-50

Cotton table cloth. Table cloths are probably the most desirable of the old linens. This is a large size and impressive in its design and hand work. The crochet work is very fine.   Value $200-300

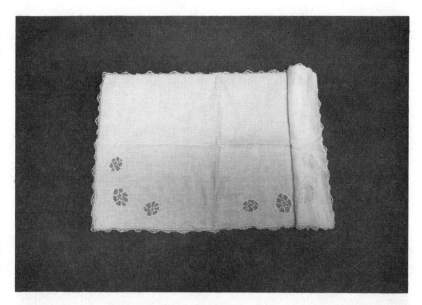

Dresser scarf 42'' long, 18'' wide, satin stitch. Edged in narrow crochet. Flower open work. Linen.   Value $35-45

Linen runner, Swedish. 41'' long with stylized Christmas trees in colors of red, green, black and orange. Before 1930.   Value $35-50

Our forebears had something for everyone, and more than enough of those somethings to fill every need, wish, time and place. This large centerpiece was intended as a "between meals centerpiece." In a piece of this kind the workmanship is important because it was basically a display piece, always on view as an attention getter. Now we seek this sort of thing to fill a nostalgic need, a time when what sat on our table between meals was a very important consideration.   Value $50-95

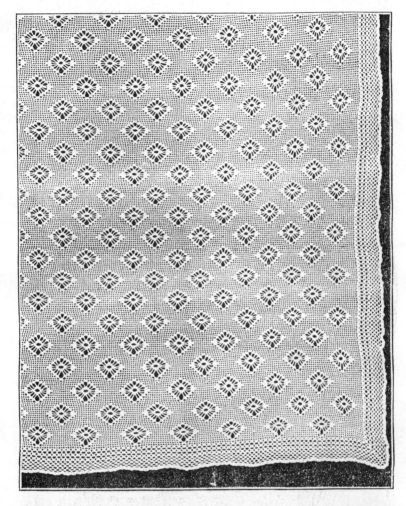

Crocheted centerpiece in an all-over diamond design. Rather monotonous but the workmanship is excellent.   Value $25-30

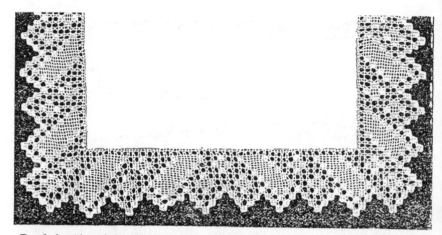

Tea cloth with wide border. The square shape with its wide border of fine crochet is aesthetically pleasing. The tea party is making a small comeback so these cloths are desirable as useful items as well as for their beauty. Value $50-65

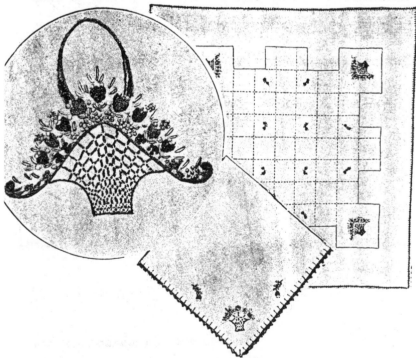

This delightful embroidery work dates from 1923. These were considered 'summer time' table sets and could be bought ready to do the embroidery work. They are now fairly easy to find and are really enchanting. The colors are usually bright and cheerful and the baskets of flowers, figures, animals or other representations are a delight to the eye. These were made of 'cream art' cotton which was practical, durable and inexpensive. This is a bridge set of cloth and matching napkins. Value of set $35-45

Ecru linen, imported from Ireland. Left: rose design with French knots; right: cut work with lace edging.

Set at left $100-150
Set at right $125-175

Top: In spite of the shortage of good hand laundries today, linen and damask tablecloths of large size are back in style. The 'Meadow Bleach' label on this linen double damask tablecloth, 72''x108'' size in the chrysanthemum pattern insures it to be "the aristocrat of linens, woven on the world famous looms of Ireland." Sometimes these cloths are found still boxed, with original labels and with the matching napkins. I own several family sets which have never been used. Satin banded.　Value of tablecloth $200-225
Value of cloth and napkins $225-300

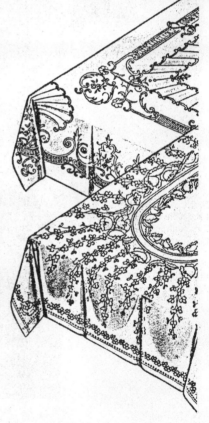

Right top: Linen damask in the 18th century pattern which is a rose and scroll effect. These linens were heavy and durable.　Value of tablecloth $150-175
Value of cloth with napkins $175-225
Bottom right: Hemstitched linen damask tablecloth in an unusual poppy and shamrock pattern. The linen in all these cloths is fine, even and close in texture. The collector should be acquainted with quality although beauty is a first consideration. Value of tablecloth $175-200
Value of cloth with napkins $225-275

Above: An oval centerpiece. The branched bars here are responsible for the lacy background which silhouettes the fruit. Linen.   Value $65-75

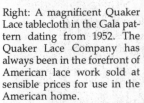

Right: A magnificent Quaker Lace tablecloth in the Gala pattern dating from 1952. The Quaker Lace Company has always been in the forefront of American lace work sold at sensible prices for use in the American home.
                    Value $125-150

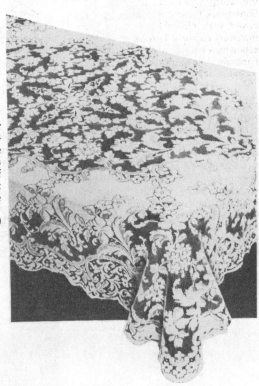

The old, well softened linen hand towel on the left is a masterpiece of Victorian white on white work. The detail is superb and the fact that it has been treasured for many years speaks of its sentimental value as well as its workmanship. These small towels are easy targets for collectors since so many of them seem to have been saved and cared for.   Value $25-35

The owner of this sacking dish towel says her mother made it for her when she was going through a "cowboy stage." The pattern was pressed on with a hot iron. The charm of these is always in the patterns and colors. In this case it proves the owner/collector was a helpful teenager as well as a discriminating "saver." 1930's.
Value $15-20

Cloth for bridge table. This is a typical example of a tremendously popular style. These are available, useful and still not expensive, but they represent quite clearly a definite time and way of life. Blue stitching, geometric design in orange and blue. French knots in center of flowers. 1930's.   Value $30-40

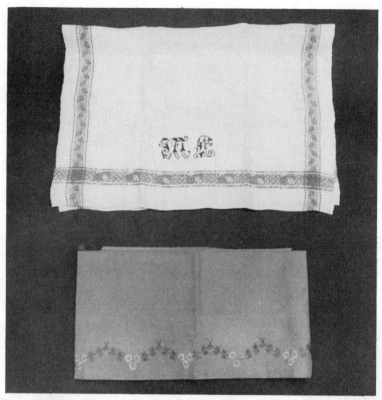

Top: Monogrammed dish towel of linen with rose colored border. This type is beautifully decorative and useful being soft and lovely to the touch. This belonged to the collector's grandmother, c. 1900-1910.   Value $20-30

Bottom: A very interesting whimsy. The end piece for a blanket or sheet, this would convert an otherwise pedestrian cover into an elaborate bed cover. Long and narrow it is blue cotton embroidered with daisies. 8'' wide, 62'' long, this is almost never recognized for what it is.   Value $35-45

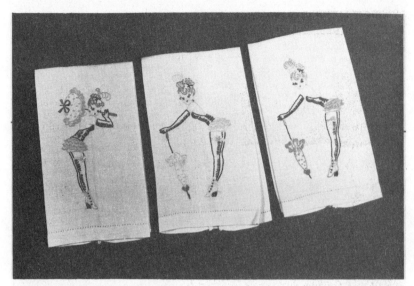

Set of 3 guest towels. "Can Can" girls are hand embroidered on stamped design. 1930s.
Value of each $10-12

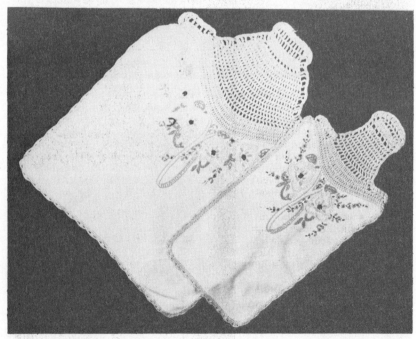

These endearing, hand crocheted and linen guest towels are wonderful accents in a contemporary bathroom. The linen is natural colored, trim is orange, the flowers are multi-colored. These are family pieces and were made in 1931. Value of set $30-35

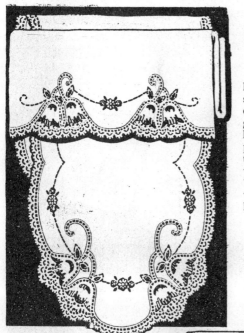

It is amazing to consider that such beauty as these pieces exhibit could have been generally unappreciated for so long. This is a bedroom set, the pillow case 42''x36'' in the tulip design. It is made of fine white tubing. The scarf, 18''x45'' is often found in white embroidery cloth, but linen was the more expensive.

Value of set $40-50

The scarf and pillow case shown here have the same dimensions but again exhibit the marvelous basket of flowers. It becomes a challenge just to document the variations in these basket designs and embroidered work sporting the baskets would make a charming collection. Crochet edging is most often found on these, but lace was also a big seller.

Value of set $40-50

Pillow case with satin stitch embroidery, hemstitched ready for crochet edging, which was never added. Early 1900's. One of a pair.   Value $35-50

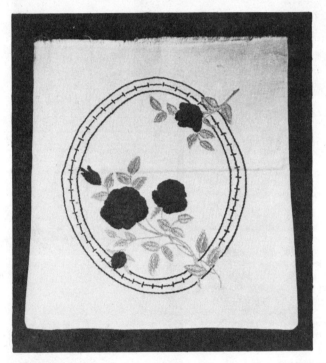

Pillow cover. Gorgeous deep red roses on heavy muslin. Green leaves, black stitched outlines. Late 1920s.   Value $20-30

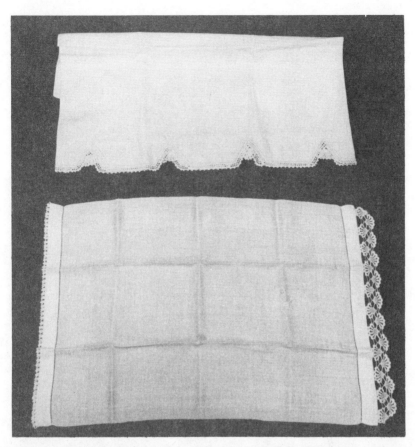

Top: One of a pair of muslin pillow cases in a somewhat different edging. There is great variety in the crochet work and laces on the old pillow cases. Each arrow here has an inset fan.   Value of pair $40-50

Bottom: One of the great old linen hand towels. This is of linen damask embroidered with the initial L. The material, as with most of these, is patterned and the very pretty crocheted edging was added by hand. Early 1900's.   Value $40-45

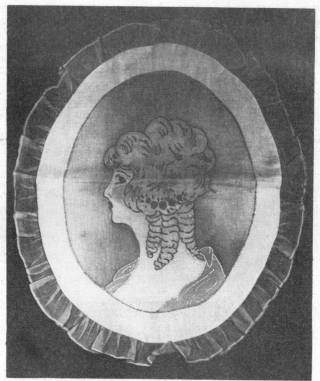

Round ruffled organdy pillow cover. Embroidered eyes and flowers in the lady's hair, otherwise hand painted in pink and silver on a blue background. 20''x18''. Late 1930s.
Value $25-28

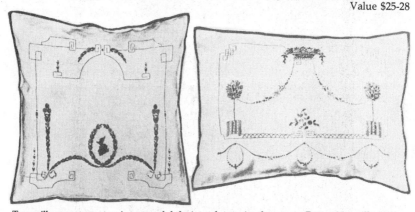

Two pillow covers – top is a graceful design of restrained rococco. Bottom is a silhouette, oblong shaped pillow which could fit beautifully into a display of one of today's silhouette picture collections. Both of these covers are done in beidermaier embroidery which was considered a novelty in 1906. It was then a revival of a 100-year-old German style, the main difference being in the materials used – instead of spangles, ribbons and beads being used on silks, satins, velvets or brocades, this 'modern' adaptation used only silk floss on soft, creamy unbleached linen.   Value left $75-85
Right $85-95

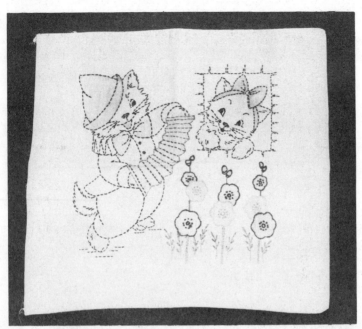

Crib pillow cover. Nicely done cat playing an accordion serenading his lady who looks over the garden. Brightly colored in black, yellow, blue, pink, red and orange.

Value $18-25

A pillow sham of Renaissance lace. Worked design. 31"x31".   Value $135-155

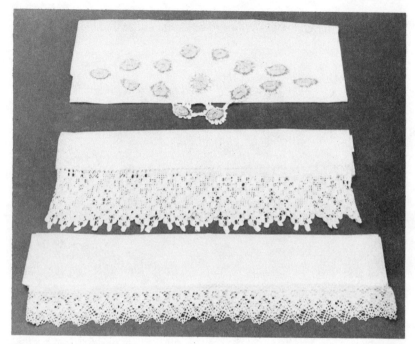

Three pillow cases each with an extravagant but highly individual trim. The top is cotton with multi colored, highly raised blossoms in a green and white bed. Very beautiful in spite of the humble quality of the case itself, and somewhat unusual trim on a pillow case.   Value of one $30-40

Center: Percale, made for the owner as a pair in 1939. So treasured a gift that they have never been used, they represent not only magnificent workmanship but that intangible important to all collectors - friendship. The lace is almost 7'' wide.
                                                                    Value of pair $45-75

Bottom: Percale case of unusually wide size. Ecru crochet trim is 4½'' wide. One of a pair.   Value of pair $40-55

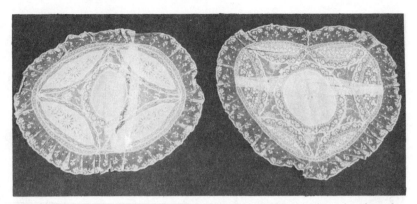

Two wonderful pillow covers, left is an oval, right heart shaped. These date from the early century and have the small button backs in the old way. The embroidery and cut work here is exquisite and these are usually displayed in a guest bedroom although they are more robust than appears. The oval is 22" long and 16" wide, the heart shaped cover is 21"x17". These are dainty, beautifully put together and very desirable.

Oval pillow cover value $100-125
Heart shaped cover value $125-150

This pillow sham matches a double bedspread. Battenberg design in center with attached ruffles which match the spread.   Value $45-55

Hemstitched pillow cases. These either boast edging of lace or crochet. The designs are surprisingly imaginative and a wonderful collection of nothing but embroidered pillow cases could be made. The basket of flowers turned up everywhere in those days, florals have a timeless appeal and the cut work has an elegance which still impresses.
Value, each, depending on amount of hand work and trim $25-35

Lovely centerpiece with its matching scarf and pillow. Irish linen flower basket embroidery and lace edging.

Value of set $55-75

Pillows continue ever popular. Those of the 1920's and '30's called 'boudoir pillows' are not a new collectible. This is typical with its shirring and heart shape. It is made of voile, has a lovely lady, French knots and ribbon and lace. Pink.

Value $20-30

This 'sofa pillow' is designed in the feather stitch. Table covers and 'scarves' can also be found with this motif which is a relatively simple technique.

Value of pillow $45-65

A scarf and cushion cover with stripes and center and end medallions of fine crochet work. A very different basket holding the bouquet. Set $35-50

This cover or 'scarf' is linen with great variety in the center and edging. The overall design makes this ideal for framing. Value $40-50

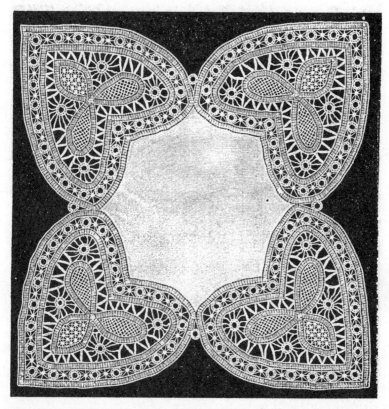

A small cover in Royal Battenberg, a lace with which most collectors are familiar. It continues to be a top favorite, and although as with the fine, older linens and laces, it is not abundant, it is nevertheless more easily found than some other types.

Value $55-77

A wonderful, realistic design in the 'oak leaf' pattern. Shades of green for the leaves, pink outlines make for a pretty sofa pillow cover. Linen.   Value of pillow $45-65

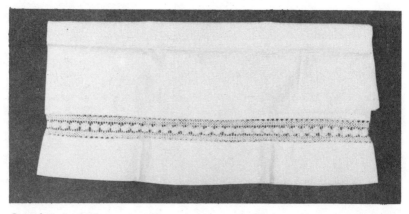

One of a pair of pillow cases with crochet insert. These were a Christmas gift in 1922.
Value of pair $45-65

Sheets with hand embroidery are much more difficult to find than the pillowcases. An old set found intact can be considered a minor treasure. These sheets are often found with colored hems. The workmanship is always good, the cut work particularly desirable. The jonquil and pond lily were favorite designs.

Value of set in excellent condition $55-75

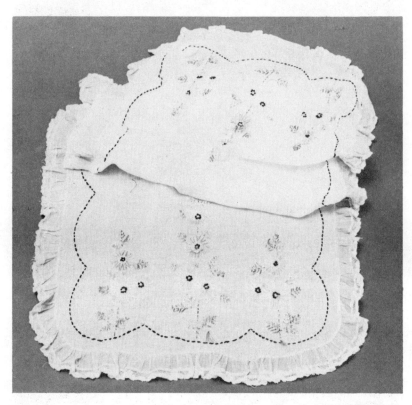

This dresser scarf matches the twin bedspread. 45" long, ecru with daisies, edged with light blue ruffled trimmed with 1½" ecru lace.   Value of set $125-175
Value of scarf $35-45

Because they are useful as well as decorative, bedspreads are among the most collectible of older, hand-embroidered pieces. The 1930's style is so definitive and eye-catching the once expensive bedspreads of the period are becoming more difficult to find and consequently more expensive.

FLORAL WREATH DESIGN

Fast color, seamless Chambray gingham is used in the stamping on this spread. It is long lasting and durable through many launderings. This classic floral wreath design complements any bed.

Value $65-85

Right: Orchid was a desirable color in the '30's and this spread reflects that partiality. This spread also came in pink or green and again features the charming 'Colonial girl.'

Value $75-100

COLONIAL GIRL DESIGN

123

Typical bedspreads of the early 1930's which are now sought after by the many devotees of that period. The measurements of single spreads of this type vary from 72x90 to 82x100 with their bolsters. Usually these are hand embroidered.

A very popular motif, the Colonial girl. Unbleached muslin with French knots and prominent 'lazy daisies.'   Value $75-95

The ever-appealing basket of flowers, this time in a medallion, unbleached muslin.
                                                                      Value $75-100

A most interesting bedspread of raw silk with heavy embroidery. Magnificent over a pink undersheet.

Value $300-400

In 1923 this was a happy setting for a little girl. Little Bo Peep on unbleached muslin on bedspread, chair covers and drapes. Left over pieces of material were used to outfit a doll. The center design of the bedspread is appliqued outlined in black. The flowers are lazy dazy natural color with blue and pink and white accents. It is almost impossible to find such a set intact. Most commonly the bedspread is to be found.

Value of spread $45-55

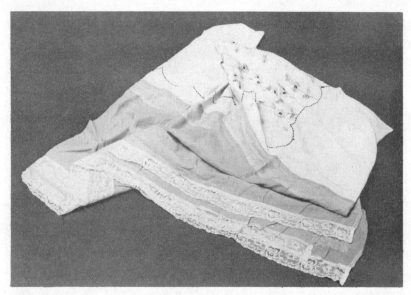

Twin bedspread in a very typical 1920's manner. Center panel of ecru lawn embroidered with pink and blue daisies with black French knot centers and a black running stitch. Side panels are light blue trimmed with 2'' ecru machine lace. Many of these are in use today to add a wonderfully light hearted air to a bedroom.

Value of spread $100-150

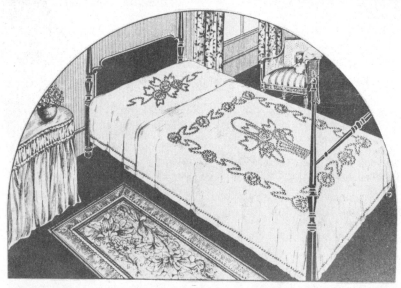

A typical bedroom of 1927. This was considered a 'simple' bedspread. Made of creamy unbleached sheeting which suggests old woven linen in tint and texture. Knot stitched and tufted, these were not heavy and easily cared for. Many have survived for us to admire and covet. The ubiquitous basket pattern. Still underpriced.

Value, single bed size $65-85

126

Ecru double bedspread. Soft netting decorated with Battenberg lace center and around the edges. Battenberg lace attaching the ruffle to the top of the bedspread. Value $250-350

Close up of darned lace border of a large bedspread. Darned lace is made of fine net and darned with white or ecru floss. An exquisite example.

Value of bedspread with darned lace trim $200-250

This square is part of a bedspread which is both beautiful and of heirloom quality. Bedspreads are among the most widely sought after of the older needlework specimens and are invariably considered prize possessions by their lucky owners. Value $200-300

With the exception of the complete lace bedspreads which are now scarce and costly, the crochet type is the apex of any collection. This gorgeous pattern in ecru in excellent condition would be valued at $300-400. The day is approaching when bedspreads such as this will be collected as are the quilts of our ancestors.

One of the great collectibles in needlework – the all crocheted bedspread. All white with a deep fringe. The amount of time these took, plus the individual skill of the maker has to be included in the ultimate value. This is a very appealing design, symetrical and beautifully done. Full size.   Value $350-450

Chair set in filet crochet. Holly and bird design. The large piece for back of the chair measures 13''x16''; 26''x11'' sized pieces for the arms. Many people today buy these appealing filet crochet pieces to frame not to use and new, machine made examples are being imported today and sold at very low prices.   Value of set $55-75

Thistles in cut-work. A chair set from 1922. Ecru linen. The simplest of bars used here.
        Value of set $45-60

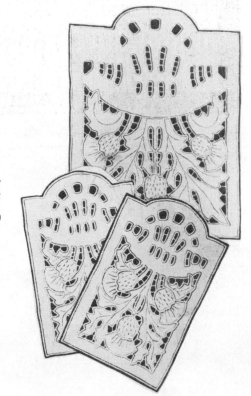

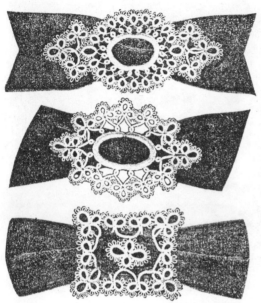

These tatted slides for collar bows are most interesting to collectors. Many times they are found in boxes of odd linens and laces and not recognized for their original use. Here they are shown as they were worn on the bows, they could be used on different bows to match an outfit. Often they are mistaken for little examples of tatting, practice pieces or pattern samples.　　Value $5-20
With original bow $20-30

Needlework was such a consuming interest in the early 1920s it was used on almost every household item. This lamp boasts a filet crochet lampshade with heavy fringe which is also crocheted. What a conversation piece this would be. The design of the lace is of the four seasons, separated by panels of flowers. The lamp itself is interesting, being an old apothecary jar.
Value of shade $85-125

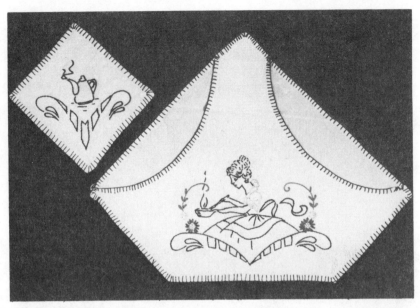

Set - napkin carrier with matching pot holder. Black stitching on white cotton.
Value $15-18

A large hand crocheted basket in pink and white. This has been framed for many years and hangs in a room devoted to sewing and sewing collectibles. 19''x14½''. Made in 1922.   Value $40-45

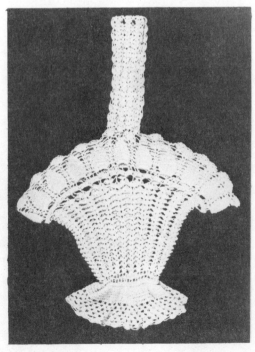

Colonial samplers have passed into the realm of expensive 'early Americana.' Collectors have other choices such as these which were the result of one of the many contests taking place just before World War I among young girls. These prize winners in one needlework contect scored first in a magazine competition and all are beautifully worked. Consider that these are already over 70 years old. The one at upper right is not strictly a sampler but a picture, however it is all hand done and skillfully worked. Any sampler of like quality and workmanship should have a beginning price of $100.

Doll's half slip. Lawn with side buttoning waist which measures 6". Hand made in 1919.
Value $40-50

These heart-shaped hanging pincushions are widely accessible and must have been made in great numbers. The crochet work differs on many of them but they are all usually trimmed with satin ribbon. They are all colorful and in a collection they are quite beautiful. Although this is typical, the trim can vary. These are among the undervalued whimsies which are not yet attracting many collectors.

Value $15-25

The whimsies of the past continue to intrigue collectors and often by their very absurdity command higher prices than some more utilitarian but more complex work. The lettuce bag is all hand crocheted and while interesting would confound any self respecting chef.

Value $20-25

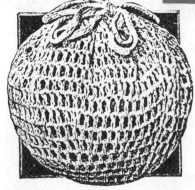

The crocheted hot water bag cover makes somewhat more sense and with its drawstring closing is rather attractive. It would be difficult for today's collector to recognize the original uses of these objects unless a previous knowledge existed. Fun additions to a collection.

Value $20-25

Whatever it was about the '20's that drives collectors into a frenzy, these little trifles typify it. The hanger cover, the flapper face hanging by a ribbon and disguising a night clothes bag, the colonial lady on the curtains and scarf set are all wonderfully nostalgic. Any or all of these is guaranteed to start a conversation. These are so widely available because they were marketed vigorously throughout the U.S. by mail order catalogue.

Hanger cover $5-10
Flapper face $15-30
Curtains and scarf set $40-50

Laundry bag for handkerchiefs and stockings in the Oriental motif so beloved in the early 1930s. Embroidered on muslin. The dress is pink and blue and is painted with embroidered accents. In 1931 when this was made the popular pattern was called "The Geishas." 24"x18".
Value $25-30

Collar and cuff case. Typical design of the 1910 era distinguished by its wonderful colors and marvelous meticulous workmanship. Deep red and yellow. Draw string closing. Lined in chintz.
Value $45-55

A lingerie case of pink satin and lace with a beautiful hand made rosette. Cases of all kinds – glove, lingerie, hosiery, handkerchief – are all becoming collectibles in their own right. This is unusually lovely. 14¼''x10''.   Value $40-45

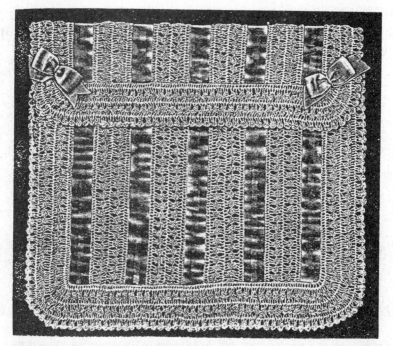

Collectors seeking to specialize would do well to seek out the various cases, which are often beautifully made, easy to display and useful. These are very feminine accessories, still affordable, vary tremendously in materials and styles. This is a hard-to-find nightdress case with the lace cover over a simply made bag and showing a profuse use of ribbon. The undercase is 14'', about usual for these cases. Value $45-55

These whimsies are gaining favor among collectors. Cases of all kinds, except those intended for pillows, are often small and easily displayed. These are made to protect silver flatware and are uncommon but delightful and worth searching for. They are made of cream linen lined with soft flannelette and bound with fast color gold bias tape. The cases marked Knives, Forks, and Teaspoons will hold 12 pieces each, the one marked 'tablespoons' hold only 6.   Set of four $35-45

This 8 piece pure linen 'refreshment set' is cream colored with a crochet edging. Four service mats and 4 napkins comprise the set. This set was meant to be used at Bridge games. Frequently these sets turn up in original boxes leading the collector to theorize that they were hostess gifts.

Set $20-25

Two card table covers. Left is made of black sateen bound in orange and is unusual with its card symbol stamping, the ubiquitous basket of flowers appears on this white linen cloth. Both of these are taped to tie at the corners.

Value, each $20-40

Picot and shell lace. This type is often found in the ever-popular ecru. It is durable lace and is often found as a finish to linen scarves. It is often found as an insertion.
Value $20-30

This is called Barred Lace and is a very simple pattern. It is easy to make and can be extended in length or width without much trouble so these sample might be found in different sizes.
Value $10-15

This is Diamond Lace and insertion. The lace is 6'' deep, insertion 3½''. This is often found on buffet scarves or bedspreads. Since a spread trimmed all around with this would be quite costly, collecting small examples can be a practical way to satisfy the collector of such beauty.   Value $15-20

This is an outstandingly beautiful lace of original design. It is delicate and light and was considered suitable (and indeed is sometimes found by Vintage Clothing collectors) on linen lawn waists. It lends itself to a cascade effect and is most often found on clothing of the period rather than utilitarian household linens. It is called Mary Bates lace after its creator.   Value $35-50

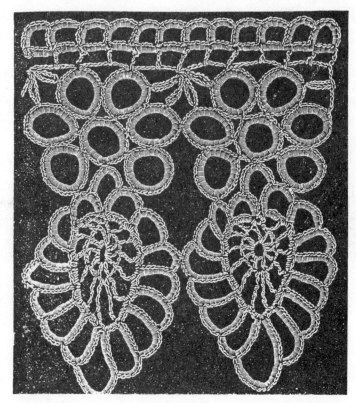

An example of Scarf Lace with Insertions. A really striking design with its medallions. This resembles reticella which was enormously popular. Value $20-25

Below: A rather typical 'dainty' lace with insertion. This was most effective with ecru or white, and the Maltese braid was recommended for Battenberg work in combination with lace. Value $15-20

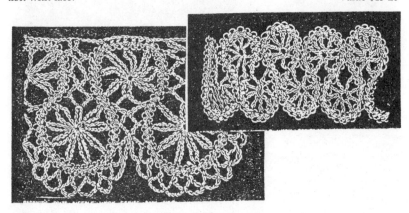

This was made specifically to adorn a sideboard 'scarf.' It is durable yet fancy and makes a handsome addition to linen.   Value $15-20

A fine example of Grape Lace made with Irish Flax and lace thread. Almost since the advent of needlework, examples of lace have been collected as mini works of art. This is not a new collectible, but it has always been a select, sophisticated one. I have seen large mounted collections of lace samples which are incredibly beautiful and often very valuable.

Value $35-45

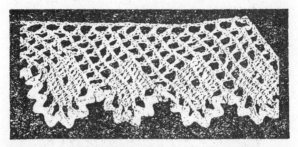

Crocheted trimmings have always held favor and are much easier to find and identify. This edging in rickrack or serpentine braid was a popular type.   Value $5-20

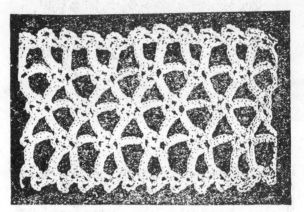

All-over lace   Value $5-20

Butterfly edge and insertion. In very fine thread this is often found on ruffle edges.
Value $5-20

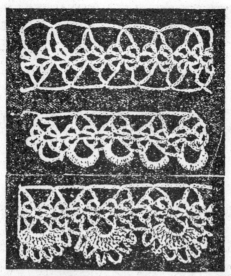

Esther edgings and insertion. Useful for almost any fancy edging.   Value $5-20

Trimming often used on clothing such as dresses or suits.   Value $5-20

It is wondrous how collecting ties together various periods and their use of various collectibles. This piece of marvelous needlework is called a 'rose mat' and was designed to be placed under a cut glass bowl. While the glass has long been sought after, it is only fairly recently that many collectors have sought the marvels of early linens and laces. This is a lovely piece.   Value $45-55

This "wheel tidy" was made with a fairly coarse thread which gives it additional body and here edges a doily. This is equally stunning on larger pieces such as tablecloths and bedspreads. Value of doily with this trim is $35-45

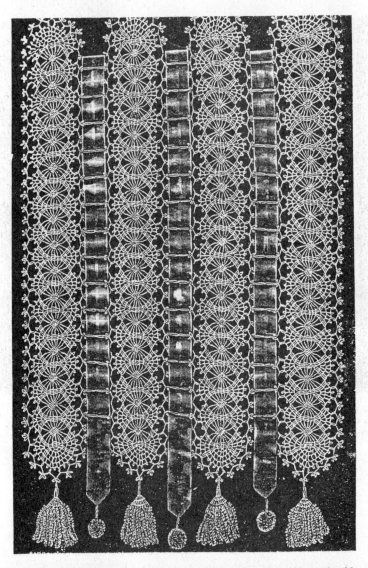

An exquisite chair back, tasseled and the pineapple motifs separated by wide ribbon. The tassels give the flavor of the period, the whole is a charming piece. Value $50-60

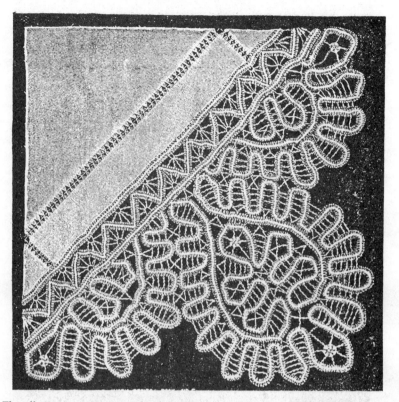

The effectiveness of this work is due to the ornamental character of the braid which gives an embossed appearance. It is quite stunning, when as shown it decorates a small cloth.

Value $55-75

An inexpensive and fairly easy way to collect various kinds of needlework is to buy small examples of as many different kinds as can be found. Here is a square for a hand made bedspread, a fine sample made before 1920. Value of this small square is $5-15

When piano scarves were all the rage, they were often bordered and inset with delicate tatting. This is 'shuttlework' a remarkably durable form of tatting. Piano scarves are most often found with fringe, those with tatting are much more difficult to find.

Sample piece $15-20

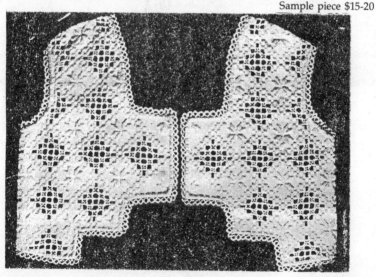

Jacket in Hardanger embroidery. Many who did this beautiful work used it exclusively for decoration on scarves, doilies, table clovers, sofa pillows and useful items for the home. Occasionally though we see an innovative example such as this bolero. A basic material that is evenly and rather loosely woven will serve as the foundation for this kind of work. This kind of stitchery is fairly simple but certainly fascinating. A jacket of this quality with such expert workmanship would be a real find.

Value $100-125

Following are samples of knitted lace dated approximately 1910. They represented a time earlier in the century when a resurgence of interest in knitted lace work occurred after a long dormancy.

Lattice Lace

Triple Leaf Lace

154

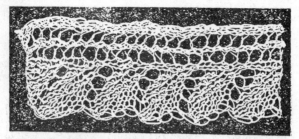

Leaf Edging

Double Leaf Lace

Single Leaf Lace

A selection of the lace edgings popular in the 1920's and '30's. Left are edgings of crochet lace. Center: Valenciennes laces in varying widths. Right: Lustrous laces of rayon. All of these were sold by the yard and demand was enormous. Interestingly, the Valenciennes so prized today was often on a par price-wise with the crochet and rayon.